My Lucky Star

My Lucky Star

ZDENKA FANTLOVÁ

Translated by Deryck Viney

HERODIAS
New York London

Published by HERODIAS, INC., 346 First Avenue, New York, NY 10009

HERODIAS, LTD., 24 Lacy Road, London, SW15 1NL

www.herodias.com

Manufactured in the United States of America

Design by Charles B. Hames
Jacket photograph by Fred Hirschmann

Library of Congress Cataloging-in-Publication Data

Fantlová, Zdenka, 1922–
   [Klid je síla, rek tatínek. English]
   My lucky star / Zdenka Fantlová.—1st ed.
      p.cm
   ISBN 1–928746–20–9
 1. Fantlová, Zdenka, 1922–
 2. Holocaust, Jewish (1939–1945)—Czechoslovokia—Personal narratives.
 3. Jews—Czechoslovokia—Biography.   I. Title.
   DS135.C97 F36413 2001
   940.53'18'092—dc21
                       00–054196

British Library Cataloguing in Publication Data
A catalogue record of this book is available from the British Library.

Published in Czech with the title *Klid Je Síla, Řek' Tatínek*, Primus 1996

Published in German with the title *In der Ruhe liegt die Kraft, sagte mein Vater*, Weidle Verlag, 1997

ISBN 1–928746–20–9

1 3 5 7 9 8 6 4 2

First edition 2001

CONTENTS

To the unknown officer in the British Army who,

through his humanity,

saved my life in Bergen-Belsen in April 1945

PROLOGUE: THE INVISIBLE MAP

The train from Prague stops at the station in a provincial town. Several people get out, hurry across the platform, melt through a passageway into the surrounding streets, and speed homeward.

Among them is an elderly woman in an autumn suit, hatless and carrying only a shoulder bag. She has no luggage. She makes her way slowly through the ticketing hall, as would someone who is in no hurry. There is no one to meet her, but she has not expected anyone. Coming out of the station, she breathes in the autumn air before stopping short at the wide steps that lead down to the street. She casts her eyes around uncertainly as if this is her first visit. Perhaps she is even a little nervous about going any farther.

At the bottom of the steps, a young lad leans on his bicycle. He watches her for a moment and decides that the woman has no idea where she is or where she wants to go.

With a mixture of curiosity and goodwill he asks, "Are you looking for someone?"

She reacts slowly, as if awakened from a dream.

"Yes, I am."

"Do you know where they live?"

"I do," she answers quietly.

"And do you know the way? If not, I can take you there."

"Thank you. You're very kind, but I can find my own way," she says, with a smile. Seeing he is not needed, the boy gets on his bike and rides off. The woman walks down a few steps and stops again.

Here on the left there used to be an institute for the blind, she thinks, searching her memory like someone snatching at a dream vision glimpsed in the ragged web of morning slumber. There had once been a lawn in front of the building, she recalls, with sandy paths and a wire fence all around. Next to the fence a blind man always stood,

*wearing the institute's uniform and playing a harmonica: a sad,
slow, unvarying tune. He must have liked it. He seemed to be playing
for his own pleasure.*

*But the blind man vanished long ago. As did the lawn with its
paths, and the institute itself.*

*She walks down the rest of the steps and makes her way into town.
She knows the route exactly, as though following an invisible map. At
times she feels she is returning from the afterlife. Everything is so familiar to her—each street, each stone—as if she were an old dog
sniffing her way. She might be invisible herself, for all the notice people take of her. At every step the scene is exactly as in the old days—
and yet quite different. She passes a cemetery where they sold candles
and asters on All Souls' Day. An inscription over the entrance had reminded visitors that the world was not their home forever:*

*What you are now, so once were we.
What we are now, you too will be.*

*She walks through a narrow gate leading into what had once been
a medieval walled town. Beyond the gate stands an inn, Na Strelnici,
Hunter's Inn, with its own theater, where a traveling company played
when it came to town.*

*She remembers how during the day the actors would take around
their posters and sell tickets from house to house for the evening show.
They were like visitors from another world. It was always a great event
when the players were in town. The auditorium was filled with
wooden benches, yet there was never an empty seat. Even children
were allowed in accompanied by a grown-up. All the old popular plays
were in the repertoire:* The Miller and His Child, Lucerna, The Fire-
Raiser's Daughter, A Night in Karlštejn Castle, *and so forth.*

*As long as the curtain was down there was a continuous bustle,
but as soon as it rose and the lights went out, a mysterious world of*

unpredictable events emerged, holding the audiences spellbound. From the stage drifted a smell of glue, makeup, old costumes, wigs, and other theatrical aromas. In its center stood a large brown prompter's box. It was hard to see around, and you could hear each sentence of the play from inside it before the actors even opened their mouths. But this bothered no one; the magic of the performance was undiminished.

It was only a stone's throw from the theater to the main square, the very center of the world. People strolled there on evenings and on Sundays, past the church, town hall, stores, savings bank, the Bata shoe shop, and the florist's shop, U Holubu, that smelled like a perfumery.

Next door to the florist's shop stood Mr. Jirsák's drapery store, where one could get snippets of material for pasting onto puppets and making dolls' clothes.

One reminiscence sets off another in the old woman's mind, like a ball of unraveling thread.

At the Štadlers' corner shop, Mrs. Mansfeldová sold not only sweets but tickets for the Lidobio, the People's Cinema. Children would sneak in secretly, wearing their Mothers' hats, to see adults-only films, like The Lives of a Bengal Lancer *and* Grand Hotel, *or a Charlie Chaplin movie.*

The woman stops in front of a new self-service store. It was not there before. In her mind's eye she sees a different picture. Here was Mr. Flajšhans, with his textiles and haberdashery. He always stood in front of his shop, intoning in an old Czech dialect, "Don't go down to the river, it's deep there, mighty deep!"

Directly opposite was the apothecary, At the Sign of the White Stork. It smelled like a hospital. One went there to collect medicine whenever someone was ill. Behind the counter was a long row of china jars with labels in Latin. The chemist in his white coat would make up the prescription, weighing out the ingredients on a tiny apothecary scale. *Next door was the grocery, where one could buy, the notice proclaimed, both homemade and imported goods. The proprietor had a cage in his back yard where he kept fox cubs. Poor things, they must have been crazy, locked up like that. He always tried to entice her in to "see his puppies."*

But she wouldn't be enticed. What she would have really liked was a bag of peanuts, but he never offered her that. So she only went to the grocer's when she had to, to buy extra fine "thrice-ground" poppy seed for the kitchen.

Next door, Stancl the confectioner had the world's best sweetmeats. She had often bought them for dessert for Sunday dinner. And what desserts they were, chocolate cream puffs, rum cake, cream tart, whipped cream rolls, marzipan potatoes with chocolate filling, and all kinds of things. Ice cream was scooped up from a china pot with a big wooden spoon.

On the corner was Mr. Tajbl's drugstore. Two huge jars of jelly beans stood on the counter, one lot white and one pink. Sometimes he would spare a few for the children.

Opposite him, in a narrow street alongside the town wall, had been a dark little shop where one had to walk up two stone steps and pull a bell string at the door. There, as a child, she would buy her fortune in a magic envelope for one Czech crown and quiver to see what the card would foretell.

Every Friday on the square there was market day. Farmers' wives came from all around to sell their butter, blueberries, mushrooms, geese, ducks, hens, and pigeons. They spread their wares out over the cobblestones on burlap—a row of butter, a row of blueberries, and so on—a different row for each. The butter came in two-pound lumps wrapped in huge green leaves, with a pattern cut on the top.

Her father's second wife used to have her own little knife for tasting the butter. She went up the line sticking it into each block, shutting her eyes and passing judgment. "No, not this one. Let's try the next." Only after trying several samples would she make her purchase.

The old woman remembers being dreadfully embarrassed and ashamed of her stepmother. She hated market day. Anca, the servant girl, had to come along with string bags, to carry home the shopping.

The biggest excitement was the monthly fair on the square. Dozens of stands were set up. One sold bags of Turkish delight, another roasted almonds. At another stand a parrot pulled horoscope cards out of a box so that people could buy one and see what fate had in store for them. Earthenware pots and pans for dolls' houses were also laid out on burlap. Next to them was a stand full of colored balloons. But the biggest draw of all was the wizened old sorceress, Klamprdonka. She sat blindfolded on a high chair in her bright skirt and black shawl, answering the questions her master put to her.

"Tell us, Klamprdonka, what has this gentleman got in the left pocket of his jacket?"

She always knew. It was real magic, and everybody clapped.

A few blocks farther on there was a big empty space called Na Pátku, where the Kludsky circus would put up its marquee festooned with colored electric bulbs. There were elephants, lions whining wearily in their cages, and a ringmaster to call in the crowds.

"Ladies and gentlemen, come and see what you have never seen before! Trained lions, an elephant dancing on bottles, acrobats performing miracles on a tightrope! Not for three crowns, not for two crowns, just one single crown! Come along, come along, you won't be disappointed!"

People poured in excitedly, scared stiff in case the acrobats fell off the high wire. There was a whiff of alien worlds about Na pátku. When the circus troupe left, the Gypsies arrived. As a youngster, she had envied them their caravans and curtained windows, their wandering from place to place. The Gypsy girls went around barefoot in long skirts with their hair flying. That, she had thought, was the real bohemian life.

If you went from the circus site along the old moat road you came to the Great Sokol Hall with its spacious playing fields. Sokol *means* falcon *in Czech, and Sokol members worked to develop this elegant bird's strength and courage. The gymnasium provided moral as well as physical exercise and even trained youngsters for the nationwide Sokol sports festivals at Strahov in Prague.*

The Sokol hall was also the center of culture and entertainment and the setting for great occasions. When she was a little girl, the famous actor Vojta Merten came from Prague to give the children a great theatrical treat, a play entitled How Kašpárek—*the traditional Czech boy hero—who rescued the Princess from the clutches of the wicked Black Magician. She had been so terrified when she saw Kašpárek starting to climb through a window into the Magician's chamber, she had sobbed aloud and run up to the stage to tell him not to go inside. Kašpárek interrupted the performance, came to the footlights, and reassured her that everything would turn out all right. When they got home afterward her brother tattled on her, and she was scolded for crying in public and holding up the show.*

The old woman walks on a little farther and she finds herself in front of a new apartment house. But what she sees in her mind is very different. This had been the garden known as Prajzler's. Inside a wooden gate, there had been rows of fruits and vegetables growing— carrots, radishes, lettuce, kohlrabi, strawberries—everything imaginable. They were for sale in a little wooden shed on one side. In front was a huge tub of water; Mrs. Prajzlerová would pull out of the produce beds whatever was asked for and rinse it in the water. One could take the food home as fresh as fresh.

Home? Why, naturally. Home is forever. The firm ground beneath our feet, certainty and order, now and forever. The whole family together. There is no other way of life. Or is there?

On she walks through the streets, past homes and gardens that have long since vanished. What has replaced them is empty space: houses pulled down to make room for street widening, a new circular road, traffic. The old stream that once flowed past, framed with willows, catkins, and pussy willows at Easter, has been filled in. New supermarkets, new notices, new people. Not a single familiar face. No one recognizes her. She feels she has strayed into the wrong town. All that is left are the low hills on the horizon and the hazy blue woods. They alone have resisted time and progress. So she was right, after all. She reminds herself why she has come and walks on to a point where three narrow streets used to meet.

On one corner had been a fire station, on the opposite one a tobacco booth. The third street led to the river. But everything has sunk into the abyss of time except for one building: her home. Rising suddenly from her memory is a large turn-of-the-century three-story house with a baroque balcony. All the neighboring buildings on both sides have vanished. This one now stands alone, a silent witness of a different age. It seems to have risen up from the very depths of her mind, long overlaid with memories of later lives spent in other lands, among other folk.

It strikes her how much this home of hers has aged. It is like meeting a close school friend years later and finding that they are now both old and gray. She can only stare. The structure is an apparition, from which plaster has fallen to reveal bare bricks. The windows are gray and dusty. The front steps are broken, and cobwebs fill the doorway. She stands silently before it as one stands by an overgrown grave that holds the remains of someone we loved.

She feels she has arrived from far away. No one ever comes out of this house now, no one ever goes in. She alone stands there, a living person watching a dead building. The longer she stands and gazes, the more confused she is by the gulf between what she remembers and what she sees. The house symbolizes something from a life long gone.

What happened there seems five centuries removed. Time itself seems unreal. Do we merely flutter along like leaves blown at random? Do we feel at home only when we have firm ground underfoot and a loved one by our side?

She feels like someone waking from a dream, confused about who she is, needing to wait a little for the scattered pieces of her life to settle in their right places.

At the back of the space where she stands is a little pile of planks. Builders have evidently left them there for tomorrow's work. She sits down on them as, in years past, she might have settled on a tree trunk felled in the forest and asks herself, How did it all happen? Where were we before we came here? Where did it all start?

My Lucky Star

1. GRANDFATHER

It really began with Grandfather, as the parish records at Cerhonice show.

Josef Mautner, originally of Blatná in southern Bohemia, made his first appearance in Cerhonice around 1865 as proprietor of the taproom of the manorial brewery in the lord's house. Later, he also leased the manorial inn at Cerhonice No. 10. He was also a corn dealer.

According to tradition, he was on close terms with the Cerhonice administrator, Father Hugo Zahnschirm. Father Hugo was a monk of the Premonstratensian order from Schlägl monastery in Upper Austria, to which Cerhonice had belonged from 1688 until 1920. In Cerhonice, the administrator, as the Abbot's deputy, represented the feudal authority.

Legend even has it that the pair of them, Mautner and the administrator, used to sit conferring together on the two celebrated oval stones in front of the Cerhonice manor house.

Despite being a Jew, Mautner not only advised the administrator in commercial matters but brokered all the affairs and appeals of the manorial staff and the common folk of Cerhonice. What Mautner said, went.

He evidently did well in the village. As early as March 15, 1868, Josef Mautner and his wife, Rosalie, bought from Jan Toman, a cottager, one part of his garden opposite the castle near the Pruhony road. In exchange for it he gave Jan Toman nine roods of good arable land in the Pod Pruhony area. This became known as Jew's Field.

On the plot he acquired, Josef Mautner built a large brick house with several living rooms, a shop, and a small reception hall. Next to it he put up a barn for six head of cattle and a number of sheds. A well was dug in the courtyard.

The shop was approached from the village green by several sets of wide stone steps. As well as having a trading license, Josef Mautner also obtained a license to sell beer, so that from 1880 onward there were virtually two inns in Cerhonice.

Mautner's taproom was in fact part of the family home, with doors leading on to the hallway, the shop, the reception room, and a small annex at the northwest corner of the building. The shop sold all manner of daily necessities. The reception hall, quite a spacious one, hosted dance evenings—musiky—up until World War II.

In 1890, Josef Mautner lost his first wife Rosalie; his second, Josefa, became joint owner of No. 50. She bore him one daughter, Barbora, or Betty, on March 21, 1897, who grew up to be a beautiful girl with dark eyes and braids rolled up into two little buns over the ears, as was the fashion. Old Mautner died around 1910.

They were a good, caring Jewish family. In the little corner room Josef's unmarried brother, Jáchym, had lain bedridden and in pain for many years, paralyzed by a stroke and tended by his sister-in-law.

The Mautners of Cerhonice came to a tragic end. From the beginning of World War I, Josefa suffered fits of deep depression. During one bout, in the spring of 1916, she left home early in the morning and ran to the Lomnice stream at Mirotice, at least two miles away, near the Karlov estate of the Schwarzenbergs. There she was found drowned in a deep pool.

Betty was left entirely on her own. She was eighteen.

2. A FATEFUL MEETING

Arnošt Fantl was a fine young man, with blond hair and smiling blue eyes, who had just started an apprenticeship in brokering iron ore to steel factories and traveled around the Blatná area visiting customers.

One day when he was bound for Cerhonice on foot, black clouds gathered in the sky. He was still in the fields when a great storm broke. Running through the rain, he could hardly see his way. At last, soaked to the skin, he made it to the first inn he could find in the village. Bursting through the door, he stood dumbfounded. For there, in a white blouse, behind the bar, stood the lovely Betty. Her black eyes rested on him for a moment. He stared back as if struck by lightning.

After he ate a meal and dried himself he knew he had to take a train back home to Blatná. When the storm passed, he persuaded Betty to accompany him to the station. She agreed, and as the train went off she stuck out her tongue at him. It was love at first sight. Arnošt knew that the beautiful Betty was the only one for him. He visited her whenever he had the time, and she fell in love with him. Apart from being so fond of him, she was no longer on her own now and had someone she could entirely depend on; in due course, Arnošt helped Betty to sell the inn property to one Anna Smolová of Malcice, with a few acres of land thrown in.

So ended the Mautner dynasty in Cerhonice. Betty moved to Blatná, and in 1918 she married Arnošt. The wedding was at the Hotel Bristol in Prague. Betty looked wonderful in white, with a veil and a wreath on her head.

The rabbi who conducted the wedding ceremony included some words of rare wisdom in his address: "Happiness," he said, "is something you will only find at home. You would be looking for it in vain anywhere else." But he hardly needed to tell them that. They were in love and blissfully happy.

They were my parents.

For their honeymoon they went to Vienna, the first time they had ever left the Cerhonice region. Vienna was all bustle, with its fine buildings, theaters, coaches, shop windows, music and culture. They were entranced.

When they returned they settled in Blatná, on the upper floor of a cottage near Blatná Castle. In September 1919 they had their first child, Jirka, or Jiríček, little Jirka.

He was my brother.

He was a sickly baby and they feared for his life. They used to lay him in the tiled oven, where it was warm, and hold a mirror in front of his face; if it misted over, that meant he was still breathing. But Mrs. Rázová, the midwife, helped to pull him through. I was born two and a half years later, a spirited little girl (I was told) and highly inquisitive. My first great experience occurred when I was three.

One Sunday there was a big event in Blatná: New bells were to be installed in the church steeple. The whole town turned out to watch. Father and Mother and Jiríček went along, but I was left at home with Grandfather. There was going to be a big crowd, they said, and little Zdenicka was too small. My disappointment was so great I thought I would never get over it. Why had I been singled out to stay home, when I was the one who was keenest of all to see the bells? How was I going to see them if I had to sit at home with Grandfather keeping guard over me?

I just had to see those bells. But time was running out. Outside, on the streets, the whole population of Blatná was watching with excitement to see how they would pull those gigantic bells up into the tower. Suddenly I saw that Grandfather had gone to sleep with his pipe in his mouth. My moment had arrived. I ran out of the room, down the stairs into the hall, and out through the front gate.

The street in front of our house that had a good view of the church was crammed with people. Though I was only knee high, I wriggled my way between them as if going through a dense forest, until I found Mother. How I knew it was her I cannot say, but it was. I pulled at her skirt until she bent down to see who was bothering her. When she saw me she was startled at first, but then she smiled and nudged Father, to show him what a brave little girl he had. With a laugh, he held me up high above the heads of the crowd and then sat me on his shoulders. And what did I see?

The bells, already hauled up to the right height, were just dropping neatly into their places in the tower. I hadn't missed it. I was beside myself with excitement and felt I had won the biggest victory of my three-year-old life. And in the end, even Grandfather forgave me for having given him the slip.

I stole something once while playing in the street, though I didn't think of it that way at the time. Mrs. Boušová ran a small grocery store next to our house. There were two stone steps leading up to it. Two sacks, tucked down to halfway, always stood on the pavement, one on each side of the door, one full of prunes and the other of peanuts. When I was playing in the street I used to move around those sacks like a kitten near a saucer of cream. It wasn't the prunes that interested me, but the peanuts. I could have asked Mrs. Boušová if I could have a few—but she might have said no. So one day I decided to get some without asking.

I ran indoors and put on a pinafore, like a good little girl, and went straight back to the sacks, I filled my pinafore pocket with peanuts, and went off to the back garden to eat them. But there was a snag. At the bottom of the garden was a dark shed with a huge ace of spades poster stuck on the wall. It depicted a creature with long claws, bare fangs, and great yellow eyes, which looked at me and knew all about me.

I was scared stiff. From that day on I never went into the shed, or around to the grocer's again.

My father often took me for walks to Blatná Castle. We had to cross a wooden drawbridge under which water lilies were growing, with leaves like lettuces. After that followed a long, long walk through the wonderful castle grounds. Those were idyllic days for a child, carefree and full of affection.

And then came a great change.

3. THE NEW COUNTRY TOWN

Early in 1925, Father decided we should move to Rokycany, a larger town with iron foundries, a rolling mill, and steel furnaces, where he could make a much better living. He was an able and hardworking man, much loved for his good humor. He longed to provide a good life for Betty, free from worry, and a better education for their two children than he had had himself. In this new town there were two elementary schools, a secondary council school, and a grammar school.

So a new stage in our life began.

The house we moved into welcomed us with open arms. It almost smiled upon us. Father installed his parents, who were getting on in years, on the second floor; we lived on the first. There was a pretty balcony over the street, and a covered gallery over the courtyard behind. The house had several rooms plus a big kitchen, with another little bedroom behind that. It seemed as big as a castle. The hall was so long I could ride my tricycle down it.

On the street side of the ground floor my father had his iron brokerage, with an office and storerooms behind it. Grandfather immediately planted himself, with his pipe, in the corner behind the counter. He occupied this seat first thing in the morning, and though there was an assistant to serve customers, he kidded himself that he was busy all day long. He only left the shop at midday to join us in the kitchen, sit down at the table, bang his fist on the table, and shout, "Let's see some food served!"

Father's business was soon established, and our new life got off to a promising start. Peace, love, and happiness reigned in the family; it never occurred to anyone that things could be otherwise. Father spent all week traveling and seeing customers, but he couldn't wait for Friday so he could come back to his family. In fact, he had found at home exactly the domestic bliss that the rabbi had talked about at their wedding. There seemed no reason to believe this family idyll wouldn't last forever.

But it was not to be.

We were struck an unexpected blow. Mother fell victim to a mysterious and unexplained malady. She started getting high fevers and no one could tell the cause. Dr. Drábek, who had visited us children whenever we were ill—I remember how cold his ear felt when I had a fever and he laid it on my chest—thought she had blood poisoning.

My brother and I went to stay with neighbors so as not to be in the way. Father would come around to see us, his eyes red from crying. I scribbled a note for Mother with my red crayon on a piece of paper, as if to say we would go for a walk together as soon as she was well, and I would take my new red umbrella.

"Yes, of course I'll give her your little letter," my father promised, and wiped away his tears.

Then things happened very quickly.

Two days later Father arrived to pick us up. Mother wanted to see us. We walked along, with Father holding us by the hand, me on his right side and Jiríček on his left. As we walked into the bedroom, Mother was lying on a pile of white pillows with her lovely brown hair spread all over them. As soon as she saw us she buried her face and started sobbing bitterly. The pain of seeing her darling children for what might be the last time was too much for her to bear.

Early the following morning she died. It was a sunny day, November 5, 1925.

She was only twenty-eight.

Jiríček was six years old, and I was three and a half.

The whole town escorted Mother to her grave. She had always shown understanding for other people and was universally loved. The death of his beloved Betynka was more than my father could bear. He could not imagine life without her. Her last words rang in his ears: "Arnošt, my beloved, thank you for the lovely seven years we have had together."

My father now conceived a desperate plan. Without her, life had lost all meaning, so he would end it. He would kill himself and take his children with him to the next world, where we would all meet again.

He found a revolver. A few days after the funeral, he made up his mind to use it. He waited until we were fast asleep, telling himself it would be easier then. He would not have to look into our eyes, so he could do what he had to do quickly and properly. First me, then Jiríček, then himself.

His decision made, he came up to my cot and pointed the revolver at me. At that moment I woke up. As soon as I saw him standing over me I gave him a big smile. He looked at me and the revolver fell from his hand. Mother must have been watching from heaven and made it happen like that; certainly she would have wanted us to carry on without her. Father seemed to hear her voice. He threw the revolver away and found in himself the strength to live.

In later years he told me how important it was to have a companion in life. "A shared pleasure is a double pleasure; a shared pain is half a pain." He said, "If you ever suffer a deep grief, immerse yourself in work. That's the only thing that can save you."

Father spoke from experience. He threw himself into his business now, working not only for himself but for the other ironworks in the area. We hardly saw anything of him. We were looked after by his old parents, who still lived in the house. But that was a temporary arrangement. He realized, though he was loath to admit it, that his parents were entitled to a quieter old age than looking after us all day. Another mother was needed. As far as he was concerned, he could not imagine having a second wife.

But his parents evidently thought remarriage was a good idea, so, he reluctantly began to look around. Several matchmakers were mobilized.

Young widower with two children seeks . . .

An unmarried clerical worker from a large respectable Jewish family in Pardubice was found, named Ella. Both her parents were alive, as well as two brothers and two sisters. The sisters, Irma and Marta, were married, and so was her older brother, Robert. Only the youngest of the family, Karel, was still single, and was therefore called Little Charlie, Karlícek. Ella had never had many offers, it seemed, and was getting on a bit for marriage. She decided to accept my father, and indeed she was fond of him. But it always remained a one-sided love.

One day Grandmother announced that a new mother was going to move in and took us to the local barber. He was told to cut my hair so that it covered only half my ears, and to give me bangs. I looked as if I had a pudding basin on my head, but that didn't worry me.

The day arrived for our new mother to introduce herself to us. She brought her own mother with her, our new grandmother.

The two of them stood at the window in one room, waiting for us to be brought in for the official audience. I was first.

There I stood in front of this strange lady who was wearing a dark blue woolen dress with a row of large white mother-of-pearl buttons running down the center. I was so impressed with those lovely shining buttons I couldn't take my eyes off them. Nothing else about the meeting interested me.

The wedding took place on June 3, 1926, at the Na Veselce Hotel in Pardubice. The couple went for their honeymoon to Smokovec in the Tatra mountains. Our new mother looked happy enough. For my father, the pleasure came from enjoying the mountain scenery and forest air.

I never had the feeling that I had a new loving mother; it was more like having a governess in charge, who ran the household and made sure we always had enough to eat and wore the right clothes.

So I really grew up on my own. We had a cook, Katty, and a chambermaid, Anca. I used to sit with them on a stool in the kitchen; that was where I really felt at home. They were fond of me and I shared all my secrets with them. One time I saved Katty's life when she choked on a piece of bread. I kept thumping her back until the lump shifted. Katty came from a German area in the Sudetenland and didn't know much Czech. When she caught her first breath she gasped:, *"Stenycko neny telala bum bum tak Kattyno pyc!"* Zdenka no go bang-bang, Katty a goner!

The following year Father sent us for a summer holiday in Pec near Domazlice, and Anca went too. I loved that. There was an area behind the hotel with little chairs and tables, so we could have breakfast out in the sun instead of in the kitchen like we did at home. Beyond that was an enclosure with a fishpond and grass around it. There were geese there but you could sit and pick the dandelions. The pond was muddy. I had rubber bathing shoes so I didn't mind much, even if it was rather squishy. Jirka and I—he wasn't Jirícek any more—used to go off on our own into the surrounding forest to collect blueberries in a painted jug.

We also waded through a cold stream that was so clear you could see the bottom. When the sun shone on it, the water glittered like silver. There were forget-me-nots on the bank, and we would sit there on the grass, watching the shiny trout dart upstream. There was a chicken yard by the hotel too, with hens and a cock. Around it was a wooden fence with a little gate. This place was strictly off limits on account of the rooster, who was supposed to be wild and dangerous. I was only five, but I was never one to miss anything, so I determined to have a look at him. One day when nobody was around I opened the gate and went inside. There was the rooster, looking around proudly as if he were the monarch of the world, while his hens pecked quietly and cackled. I started running after him. At first he circled away from me but then, suddenly angry, he turned around, flew in my face, and grabbed my neck in his claws. I shouted at the top of my voice. Several people rushed from the hotel. Seeing what was up, they caught the bird and dragged it off me. The hotel owner was quite beside himself. It might have pecked my eyes out.

We had a telephone in the office. In homes such things were still rarities, but for businesses they were indispensable. Our phone was a big black instrument attached to the wall. First you had to take the receiver down off the hook. Then you turned a handle on the side and the exchange answered. Our telephone number was 5.

One day Father called me into the office to talk to somebody on the phone. It was Mother, calling from Prague to tell me I had a new baby sister.

I felt rather as if I had been given a new toy. I couldn't wait for her to be brought home so I could put her in her carriage and take her for a ride in the town square where everyone could see her. After that I would play with her in the house.

Father took us to Dr. Boruvka's home in Prague. Mother was in bed and next to her, in a cradle all cushioned and curtained, lay a little creature with black hair and the tiniest hands and fingers I had ever seen. They decided to call her Lydia.

When Mother arrived home with the baby, everything turned out differently. My dreams of pushing my little sister in a carriage were dashed.

A private nurse was hired, a German called Sister Gaube. She wore a light brown nurse's uniform and a matching veil with a white headband. The little baby was entirely hidden from view in a white wicker cradle, behind a frilly white curtain.

Sister Gaube was very strict and wouldn't let me go near the cradle. I couldn't understand why and felt shut out of everything. They managed to kill all my love for the new child, all my interest in her. So I dug in my heels. I stopped asking to see her, showed no further interest, and turned my back on her.

I was rescued from this crushing childhood disappointment by the next stage in my life—maybe the most important of all.

4. SCHOOL

On September 3, 1928, Grandfather took me to school for the first time. The school was in one of the parish houses, standing on a small estate just behind the church. Our grade, IA, was on the second floor, up a wooden staircase worn thin over the years. We were greeted by the teacher assigned to the class, Anna Sedláčková. She was to become the most important influence in my life. I respected her and acknowledged her as on a par with my father, and she guided me carefully and conscientiously from first grade right up to fifth.

If school is the foundation for life, Anna Sedláčková certainly laid it carefully. She taught us not only reading, writing, and arithmetic but an affection for poetry and the Czech language itself. I sat in the front row, taking in every word she said. I loved school, and I loved her.

Anna lived close to us and passed our home on the way to school. From half past seven on I would be waiting for her to carry her bag of books. She was tall and slim, of an age I could only guess at—more on the older side than the younger, I judged. She combed her dark hair straight back and tied it in a knot behind. She was always kind and helpful and took her role as teacher and mentor seriously. I learned quickly and always did my homework properly, mainly to please Anna.

Our school had a special charm in the wintertime. It was still dark when we set off from home, but there were already lights in the school windows to welcome us and the stove had been lit to make the classrooms pleasantly warm. In fact, I felt happier at school than at home. My bench neighbor was Vera, and the two of us became best friends. She was an only child and I felt like one—Jirka had his own buddies—so we took to each other like sisters.

Vera lived just on the other side of our courtyard. I had only to run along a path and I was already in her cottage. Her father was a men's and boys' outfitter and a keen Sokol gymnast. He marched in processions wearing the Sokol uniform, a cape tied with a cord, high boots, and a Sokol cap with a feather in it. Vera's mother baked the most marvelous cakes on a greased griddle, dusted with cinnamon. Her father used to run around from the workshop with his measuring tape hanging around his neck and down five of them at a go. She also used me as an example for her own daughter.

"Look how nicely Zdenicka does her hair, Verunka. And you go around looking like a scarecrow!"

I was made more than welcome in their home. Whatever Vera did, I did too. If she wore a white dress and carried a little basket of roses on Corpus Christi at Easter, her mother would find me a white dress and basket of petals too, so I wouldn't feel left out and could join the procession with Vera. I wasn't afraid Mother would see me on this Christian holiday, because she never went to that kind of event.

I felt very important, walking alongside Vera and scattering petals in a circle around me along the path to Calvary, where we stopped at every turning in front of the figures of the Holy Family. After the procession was over I went back to Vera's to change and then home quite innocently, as though nothing had happened.

We both joined the Sokols and were keen on sports. We used to go to the Áleje sports center together, where there was an athletic field with a running track and a weed-overgrown tennis court. We got hold of a couple of rackets, each with at least three broken strings, and some worn out tennis balls. To fix the rackets we crocheted little red nets from pieces of wool. We played for all we were worth, shouting the scores in English (even though we didn't understand the words) and pretending to be world champions.

Close by the Áleje was a swimming hole. There were several wooden bathhouses with the knots in the boards poked out, and a small hole called the Great Pool, fed from the dam by a little stream. We would blow up our yellow water wings, put them on, and lower ourselves down the slippery wooden steps into the stream.

The bottom was muddy and the banks were overgrown with willow trees and willow herb. We jumped along on one leg, pushing the water to each side with our arms, and so learned a kind of breaststroke. Only after that did we have the courage to go into the Great Pool, feeling we had passed a great test of maturity. The only annoying thing were the swimsuits, which in those days were always woolen, never dried properly, and felt horribly itchy.

In the winter we explored the low hills nearby on heavy wooden skis and imagined we were in the Alps. Sometimes we careened down the slopes on these skis, sometimes on sleds.

What we enjoyed most of all was skating on the fishpond. Our skates were of the kind that fitted over the shoes and were tightened with a key, which you had to keep in your pocket. First we cast a discerning eye over the ice to see if it was thick enough to support us. Then we sat down on a log, put on our skates, which had spiral toes like violin scrolls, and tightened them with a key. Now we were ready to go. We learned to make forward and backward turns and even to jump from one foot to the other like Sonja Henie in the newsreels.

Winter was lovely, and summer too. And so were spring and autumn. Our life was spent in the open air, in the forests and meadows along the rivers and ponds. We were more out of doors than in.

But then elementary school ended and grammar school began. Before the end of term, Father bought a leather-bound blank book and wrote one of his bits of wisdom in it:

Never envy, never slander, never despair,
wish well to all, work hard, and hope.

He always followed his own advice.

I asked Anna Sedláková if she would write something also. She said she would be pleased to. She took the book home with her and, when she had finished her contribution, asked me if she could bring it to our house. Of course I agreed, feeling quite overwhelmed by the honor.

When she rang our bell my heart was thumping with excitement, as if God himself were on the doorstep.

She was sitting in Father's armchair when she handed me the book. I thanked her over and over again. She had written in her calligraphic hand the following verses:

> *Life hastens on, and we are scarce aware*
> *how, pace by pace, we too are hastening.*
> *Today, tomorrow, both evaporate*
> *as winter follows summer, autumn spring.*
>
> *The world around is changing at every step*
> *and we ourselves strange alterations know;*
> *smiling today, tomorrow we shed tears,*
> *and where flowers bloomed at dawn,*
> > *the night brings snow.*
>
> *One more year passes and we shall forget,*
> *and feel the frozen dew of indifference*
> *behind us, like a gravestone, earthward fall.*
>
> *These things alone—the nursery tales we learned,*
> *and those dear ones who loved us—these alone*
> *always, and gratefully, we shall recall.*

5. JEWISH HOLIDAYS

There were only a handful of Jewish families in our town and in the surrounding area, living the same kind of life as everyone else. They all had their own jobs, offices, businesses, farms. Their children went to the same schools, spoke Czech, joined in Sokol gymnastics, and had lived on Czech soil as long as they could remember. They did not feel superior or inferior to the rest. They didn't follow Jewish dietary laws; they ate the same food and drank the same beer.

It was only the religious holidays that were different. They did not have Christmas trees nor go to church for midnight mass nor join in the Corpus Christi procession—except for me, who enjoyed it in secret as a piece of theater—but they observed their own Jewish holidays. There was one around Eastertime, Pesach. In the autumn was Rosh Hashana, the Jewish New Year, and Yom Kippur, the Day of Atonement. Each one had something to do with food, and that was all they meant to me at the time. Either there was a great feast or nothing at all. On Yom Kippur we weren't allowed to eat or drink anything for twenty-four hours. I wasn't clear why, and I used to sneak back home for a bite.

For me it was a different kind of holiday. Our Katty and Anca always baked potato fritters in the oven that day, red and crunchy, something we never had at any other time. I looked forward to the Day of Atonement all year. There was no synagogue in our town, only a little prayer room. This was a simple first-floor room, set aside and furnished for prayer. There was a raised desk on which the torah lay open between two scrolls and was read from in Hebrew. The visiting rabbi used to point to the words with a long silver pointer in the shape of a hand. In between readings he would sing sad melodies I had never heard, in a language I didn't know, quite different from anything I had come across in school. Behind the desk was a casket with a heavy curtain embroidered in gold and silver thread. On either side in front of the platform stood a row of benches; men sat on the left, women on the right.

Grandfather, as one of the older generation, observed all holidays scrupulously. He went to the prayer room wearing a tallis, a white shawl with black stripes, over his shoulders. And he really did pray.

Father kept the holidays too, not so much for tradition's sake as Grandfather did, but more out of respect for him. Or perhaps they meant something to him. I don't know.

For Mother, the Jewish holidays were like two milestones dividing the calendar: one in the spring, one in the autumn. Those were when you did the big washing and cleaning and got ready for a major feast. On festival days she went to the prayer room, but more as a social event than out of piety. She had her prayer book open on the rest in front of her. It was supposed to be read Hebrew style, from right to left. But the womenfolk just gossiped about children and household matters.

At Yom Kippur, when everyone was meant to be fasting, it was the custom to take into the prayer room for each mother a fresh apple stuck with cloves. The idea was to sniff them to avoid fainting from hunger. That was something else I looked forward to each year, so I could make pretty patterns with the cloves.

My only objection to the Jewish holidays was that I wasn't allowed to go to school on those days, and I had to wear my best clothes, Sunday clothes, even if it was a weekday. This made me feel excluded and I felt I was being pointed at and told to stand apart, all for no reason. When my schoolmates passed by they stared at me as if they had never seen me before, and I didn't belong among them—even though I was the same person I was the day before. I hated this invisible gulf separating me from the others.

. . .

One day Father announced that we were going to have a motorcar. They were still a rarity; people traveled by train or bicycle or went on foot. But buy a car he did, a brand new Peugeot. There it was, standing quietly in front of the house, painted green, with huge mudguards and mica windows that were hard to see through. Father was wearing a chauffeur's uniform bought for the purpose, including large goggles tied with elastic and big chauffeur's gloves with cuffs up to the elbows.

One had to turn a crank in front to start the motor.

The whole family set forth in style for a Sunday outing. We had been thinking what fun it would be to drive out into the countryside in our own car. But we didn't get far. It started raining, and suddenly the whole car lurched to one side. A wheel had come off and rolled away into a potato field.

We all had to get out. Jirka and I went to look for the wheel among the potatoes. Meanwhile Father was bent double, like a mushroom picker, searching the road for the lost nuts and bolts so he could put the wheel on again after Jirka and I had located it. There was no one else on the road, and in the end Father managed to get the parts together. We got in and drove home again, dirty and sopping wet.

Mother complained that there'd been no need to drive anywhere at all. Her remark quite ruined Father's pleasure. Ever since then I have distrusted cars and preferred to walk where I could and go by train for longer distances.

6. RITES OF PASSAGE

When I was eleven I started grammar school, which brought fresh worries: more subjects, less time for playing out of doors, and a new disturbing element. There were boys in class for the first time. This upset our equilibrium. Each of us was enamored with one of them. Or, as it was usually put, "*She's* mooning about Tom, *she's* mooning about Dick," and so on.

We either sat giggling on the benches or sent each other secret notes. It was all very exciting, and our schoolwork suffered accordingly. To be escorted home by one's chosen gallant was pure ecstasy. On Sunday mornings we dolled ourselves up to parade around the main square in the hope that he would appear too. There was a garrison in the town, and if junior or even senior officers turned up the promenade became very colorful and thrilling, with much exchanging of coquettish glances.

It wasn't long before I fell deeply in love for the first time. I was twelve. During the summer holidays Father dispatched Jirka to a scout camp, while Mother, Lydia, and I were sent to Novi on the Yugoslav coast. The Adriatic Sea—not just a fishpond in the countryside! I couldn't wait to see it. Mother got the local seamstress, Mrs. Kuchlerová, to make us some beach outfits, which we called "beach pajamas" because they looked so much like regular pajamas. Two pairs for each of us, one pale blue and one pink. That was the fashion.

Having them made was torture. I had to stand still so long, I felt I would pass out each time Mrs. Kuchlerová slowly pinned the sleeves onto my clothes, marked the length with chalk, and fitted the sailor-boy collar. These visits put me off the holiday and the seaside idea altogether.

We went by train, a very long journey. I had a window seat. Suddenly in the distance I had my first glimpse of blue sea. A mysterious new world opened up for me. We stayed in a lovely big hotel with a room and balcony overlooking the sea. We had our own cabana on the beach. The sand was so hot that we had to wear beach shoes the whole time. The water was warm, the sea stretched out forever and I couldn't take my eyes off it.

There was a beach promenade a mile long in front of the hotel. All the guests walked there every evening. Lydia, who was only six, walked with my mother, but I was twelve and walked by myself. I had other things on my mind.

There was a young boy going up and down the promenade, with a red scarf around his neck attached to a large wooden tray laden with variously colored goodies: candied fruit, caramel apples, and lollipops. As he sold them to the visitors he recited strange rhymes in a language that sounded like Czech, but wasn't. It was a kind of song with a rhythm but no tune. He had black eyes and a dusky complexion. I fancied him terrifically. Rajko was his name.

Once when Mother stayed behind in the hotel I sneaked out onto the promenade to help Rajko sell his wares. I learned his words by heart and had them so pat that no one could tell I wasn't a native.

We would walk along side by side, singing:

Mindoli mandoli
karameli
kysely vesely
london bonbon
ris paris
aaafrika paaaprika
cuc na bidylku . . .

Lots of people came up to buy, and Rajko's sales spiraled.

One day he took me by the hand and walked quietly with me across the sand to the water's edge and back again. There was a great white ship on the horizon, and I imagined us sailing away on it one day, into the unknown, just the two of us.

My dream of bliss sank below the horizon along with the white ship, for the next day Mother, Lydia, and I were on our way home again. The new school year was about to start. Yugoslavia had been paradise.

By the time we got back from our holiday I felt very sophisticated. Vera and I decided it was high time we learned to smoke and behave like grown-ups. "Let's have a go," we agreed.

At the first opportunity, when our parents went off to Prague for a couple of days, we decided to take action. We bought a packet of Vlasta cigarettes at U Sykoru, the nearby kiosk. That was ten cigarettes, more than enough. To create a cozy atmosphere we settled down in the little room in our house, drew all the curtains, lowered the lights to make it like a night club, and put "Ramona" on the phonograph. Then we wound it up and put on the needle.

Sentimental music filled the room. Solemnly lighting our first cigarettes, we crossed our legs and felt like film stars, albeit coughing film stars. At the end of her first cigarette Vera was sick, but we had passed our first test of maturity.

In the new school year I started taking piano lessons. We had an old Hayek grand piano at home that had been part of Mother's dowry. No one played it. It was out of tune, and some of the keys had gone yellow like old teeth. As luck would have it, there was a German piano teacher in our town, a Professor Kurzová, who went to Prague twice a week to teach at the Conservatoire. She was the wife of a neighborhood doctor.

Professor Kurzová only accepted a small number of pupils, but she agreed to take me on. There were two Förster pianos in her place, an upright for students and a grand for herself. She was a follower of the old German school of classical music and taught accordingly. Technique was the be-all and end-all. Scales—upward and downward—in all positions and modes: major, minor, chromatic. She was very strict, but I enjoyed the lessons and spent hours practicing. Though I made good progress, Mother had a low opinion of my musical ambitions. Every time I sat down to practice she would drive me away, shouting, "There you go tinkling the ivories again. Why don't you darn some socks or go through your drawers? That'd be more useful."

But I had an answer to that. So as not to have to give up practicing I put on woolen gloves and carried on, hoping my mother wouldn't hear me.

I had a lot of backing from my father, though. He was very musical and had perfect pitch. He played the violin excellently without sheet music, just by ear. He often came up behind me at the piano, picked up his violin, and played duets with me. That was a real joy.

Sometimes I would tell my father that this or that piece was too hard for me to learn.

He always cut me short. "Never say something's too hard to learn. Tell yourself that if a circus elephant can learn to walk on bottles, you can train yourself to do anything. If you really want to, that is."

Father always looked on the bright side of everything and was wonderful at telling stories about his travels or his experiences in the army during World War I.

There was one moment in the day when we were all together: at precisely seven o'clock at the dinner table. Nobody was allowed to miss dinner and punctuality was the law. This was the occasion for Father to tell his stories. He put a lot of humor into them, as well as pieces of wise advice, often aimed at me. I was his favorite, partly, no doubt because I reminded him most of his beloved

Betty. People often used to say, "Just like her mother!" and look in my direction.

"Never try to have too much of anything in life!" he said on one occasion. "Just see that you have what you need and a little more. That's good enough. When you die, all you will take with you is what you've given to other people."

Another time he said to me, "You'll meet all sorts during your life. Form your own judgment about them—not by how they earn their money but by what they spend it on."

In my case his words fell on fertile soil. Even if I didn't understand them at the time, they germinated like seedlings and came into blossom later.

"Look around you, observe, learn, and educate yourself. We are put here to develop and perfect ourselves as much as we can, not to climb social ladders. They don't lead anywhere. Remember, if a dwarf climbs even to the highest mountaintop, he is still a dwarf."

In his own business, too, Father was courageous and full of enterprise. Sometimes he had ideas that were well ahead of his time. He got interested, for example, in the possibility of producing gasoline from our native coal. The more he thought about it, the more convinced he was that there were ideal conditions in our country for achieving this.

Why not start with the huge deposits around Moravian Ostrava, near the Polish border? He probed and probed. He who seeks shall find. A few other specialists were needed, and soon enough they turned up. One was a first rate Berlin research chemist, another a well-known Prague barrister. All three were convinced of the merits of the scheme and felt sure this revolutionary new source of gasoline would come into being.

They formed their own company, with Father as the main source of financing. Mother was against it. She said it would lead nowhere and Father ought to forget it and stick to his own trade—iron.

The plan was sound in theory but impracticable, and the company went bust. The German chemist escaped back to Berlin, the Prague barrister shot himself, and Father lost a lot of money.

"I told you so," Mother said.

But he never despaired, or even repented. "That's how things go in life. If you take risks you must count on sometimes losing."

He threw himself into the iron business again and soon recouped his losses.

During our teenage years we loved wandering in the nearby woods with their smells of moss and fungi and their carpets of blueberries and wild strawberries in the sun-warmed clearings. We would lie in the soft grass and listen to the birds making conversation in the treetops. The world was lovely, life was secure and went merrily on its way. On top of that, we had started dancing lessons so as not to be behind when we grew up and became ladies. All was excitement and preparation.

Materials had to be bought. Ribbons. Dresses had to be sewn, new shoes tried on. New hairdos: they were the worst. Mother took me to the hairdresser on the town square, Mrs. Hejrovská, to have my hair waved. First she wound it around little tongs that had been laid on a kerosene stove to be heated up. The hairdresser tested their temperature first on newspaper.

They were so hot the paper always burned. Having made tight curls all over my head, she then took the big tongs for squeezing the hair into waves. One wave to the left, one to the right, one to the left again, and so on. During this process she held the hair with a large comb, pressed it into waves with the tongs, and finished the coiffure with a mass of combed-out curls.

As my hair was naturally straight and thick, these sets never lasted long. Mother decided it would be best if I had a perm. This was a lengthy and rather frightening procedure. First they wound my hair around little rollers. I could see something hanging down from the ceiling like a medieval instrument of torture, waiting to be used on me. It had thin rubber cables, like black snakes tipped with clips, all hanging from a candelabra-like ring. The clips were attached to the rollers with my hair wound around them, and then the electricity was switched on. I sat paralyzed in my chair, plugged into the ceiling and abandoned to my fate.

If something caught fire, I thought, I wouldn't be able to free myself; I would burn to cinders. Various other disastrous variations flitted through my head. After a long wait they released me from the instruments of torture and took off the clips and rollers. It looked as if I had a frizzy sheepskin on my head.

On the following evenings I went to the dancing classes held in the Great Sokol Hall. In one corner there were boys standing in tight suits with polished boots and hair stuck down with Bryl Cream. The girls were in another corner. We all eyed one another to see who had the prettiest dress and who was wearing a bow. The mothers and chaperones sat on chairs along the wall, watching us critically and waiting to see which boy would come to sweep away their treasure.

Mr. Kalivoda, the dancing master, arranged us in pairs and the music struck up. He introduced us to various combinations of step and rhythm: fox-trot, slow waltz, tango. We skidded on the polished parquet floor, and the boys trod on our new shoes. By the end of the evening one could see the outlines of their sweaty hands on the backs of our new dresses. The dancing class culminated in the final lessons and a cotillion—which meant one more dress—and then the season was over.

7. PRAGUE

Except for her sister in Kolín, Mother's entire family lived in Prague. Twice a year we journeyed to the capital to visit Grandmother.

Great excitement, busy times. The day before the journey was spent gathering food to take with us, so as not to die of starvation on the way. We took a hamper full of cutlets and gherkins, hard-boiled eggs, buttered rolls, fruit, and lemonade. We had to get up before daybreak as the distance to Prague was so long—forty-five whole miles. My brother, sister, and I stood to attention on the platform in our Sunday best, while Mother bought the tickets at the counter.

The stationmaster, a stocky little man with a weedy mustache, paced up and down the platform holding a huge bell and watching for the first sign that the Prague train was approaching. As soon as he saw steam above the trees, he clutched his bell tight and reeled off the names of all the stations as far as Prague.

When the train arrived we climbed up the steep steps, Mother found a free compartment, and immediately we were told to eat. The train had its own special smell of soot and cigarette smoke, and we were not allowed to have the windows open to avoid getting cinders in our eyes. After half an hour we reached Beroun, where platform vendors were crying "Hot frankfurters, lemonade, newspapers!"

When the Smíchov tunnel approached we knew it was time to prepare to arrive in Prague—putting on our jackets and, worst of all, our gloves. Those white gloves were made from sharp cotton needlepoint and were uncomfortably tight round the fingers. I hated Smíchov. Then came Prague—the Wilson Central Station with all its noise and bustling crowds, luggage, porters, and newspaper vendors. Prague belonged to the outside world.

At Grandmother's the table was already set with a coffee service and in the middle, awaiting us, stood a *bábovka* cake sprinkled with sugar and set with almonds.

All Mother's relations were there, housed together in a great four-storied building on Tynská Street, one family to each floor.

There were three boy cousins our own age—Harry, Péta, and Bedrich. They had brought their own toys and we played all kinds of games together while the grown-ups chatted about family matters and made other adult conversation.

The next day we had to accompany Mother to the Boulevard Coffeehouse on Wenceslaus Square, where all the other aunts were gathering. There were at least five of them seated at a single round table on the first floor behind a window, like a tableau. They always greeted me with the same words:

"My, hasn't she grown! So what's new at school?"

I never knew what to say. I was much more interested in what was going on around me. The coffeehouse was humming with noise and movement, people coming and going, talking and laughing. Frock-coated waiters threaded their way through clouds of cigarette and cigar smoke, balancing trays of coffee and cakes, canapés, and other delicacies. A small page boy in red uniform, with gold buttons and a little fez on his head tied with elastic under his chin, walked between the rows of tables holding up a name card on a stick and announcing that the person in question had a telephone call:

"*Doktor Neuman k telefonu! Doktor Neuman k telefonu!*"

And a moment later he would be calling for someone else.

If it was raining on our way back, we could see the scrolling lights of the evening paper *Vecerní Ceské Slovo* reflected in the asphalt of the Wenceslaus Square, as the letters chased across the facade of the newspaper building, vanished, and reappeared endlessly. Cars, lights, people, shop windows, trams, splendid buildings, the Vltava River with the Hradcany Castle looming over it—Prague was one big dream, a world of its own, quite different from the one we knew.

It was then the clouds began to gather. In 1933, reports had started to filter in from Germany—a country as distant from our own as if it were on another planet—about the new political order being established there by the new chancellor, Adolf Hitler. The radio had broadcast several of his demagogic speeches. He sounded to us like any other fanatic, bawling and threatening. His followers and his brown-shirted storm troops multiplied day by day, but nobody we knew took him seriously. Mother hated listening and Father totally ignored him.

"No need for us to bother about him," he said. "We're no longer part of the Austro-Hungarian Empire. Although we understand and speak German, this is not Germany. Hitler is in Germany. This is the Czechoslovak Republic. President Masaryk is in charge here, and no country in the world has a better statesman at the helm."

Life went on as usual and people forgot about Germany again.

On Easter Saturday I was in a crowd in front of the Parliament building in Prague, waiting tensely for Papa Masaryk to appear. I had never seen him in person, only the portrait that hung in my elementary school and my grammar school and graced every public building in the country. Just before midday there was a murmur in the crowd and then a shout of "Here he comes!"

And it really was he, President T. G. Masaryk himself in his familiar white suit, on horseback. He jumped down and ran as nimbly as a youngster up the front steps of the Parliament. I caught my breath, seeing him with my own eyes, our one and only Papa Masaryk, handsome as a living statue and yet somehow unreal, visionary.

I wept with joy and excitement. It was an experience no one could ever rob me of. I felt privileged above the citizens of all other nations in being a child of Masaryk's Republic.

Soon afterward we became accustomed to seeing another portrait alongside Masaryk's—that of Edvard Beneš, who became the new president of the Republic in 1935 when the aging president retired. Nothing had been lost, quite the opposite. We had two strong watchdogs now, one in the forefront and one on guard behind. But, on September 14, 1937, Masaryk died. Our whole nation wept over the loss of this great man, our President-Liberator. We all felt we would never see his likes again.

We stood in the window of an apartment near Wilson Central Station and watched the train carrying his coffin—a low pedestal in an open wagon—on its way out of Prague to his last resting place in Lány. As it passed close to us people knelt and some prayed—not only for his soul but for our country and its fate. When his coffin left, it was as if the last days of free Czechoslovakia were departing.

8. DR. MANDELÍK

We didn't arrange any big journeys in 1938 and the summer holidays were divided between picking wild strawberries and mushrooms in the woods, swimming in the river, and playing tennis at the Áleje.

It was stiflingly hot and the roads were dusty.

Mother decided to send me off for two weeks to her sister Irma in Kolín, east of Prague. That was something to look forward to. My cousins Pavel and Vera took me to the baths on the River Elbe. After swimming we spent the rest of the afternoon playing tennis at their club. On one occasion I was the last to leave and wasn't sure how to get back to their house.

A stranger came up to me after he had finished his game. He struck me as pretty old, about twenty-eight, with auburn curls and spectacles. Seeing me standing at the gate looking so helpless, he asked if he could drive me home. I said thank you, and certainly, I'd love him to. His car was a big black Hudson.

I was home in no time. I had to promise him that we would go to Spa Podebrady together the next day for five o'clock tea with dance music. It all sounded very enticing and romantic. Aunt Irma saw us get out, and when I reached the house she was beside herself with excitement.

"Do you realize who it was who drove you home?"

"One of the locals," I answered. "He didn't tell me his name."

"But that was Dr. Mandelík!" she burst out breathlessly.

Her voice was trembling with awe and admiration, as if I had been escorted by the heir to some royal throne, and she looked reproachfully at this Cinderella who wasn't even aware of the honor she had been paid.

The Mandelíks were a wealthy family from Ratbor near Kolín whom everyone looked up to as the local gentry. Their sugar factories supplied the whole republic, and foreign customers too. Originally, there had been three brothers, one of whom lived with his family in Ratbor and organized production. Another was in Prague in charge of distribution, and a third in Paris.

The Ratbor brother, Otto, and his wife, Olga, had a son, Bernard, and a daughter, Hana. Bernard was my new chauffeur. He already had a doctorate in chemistry and was supposed to take over the production technology and the refineries some day. They lived in a grand mansion.

There was a very tense atmosphere in Aunt Irma's household that evening on account of my new acquaintance. She lost no time in ringing my mother to tell her that her daughter had made a good match—as if it were all settled and despite the fact that I didn't even know the gentleman's name. "Well, well, who would have thought she was up to it?" my mother retorted, with mild irony.

All the same, she could not resist passing on the family news immediately to other relations and enjoying a little glory as mother of the bride-to-be.

The intriguing news caused no little stir; everyone embellished it somewhat, and within twenty-four hours it was being repeated as a fait accompli. "Have you heard the latest? Zdenka is going to marry one of the Mandelíks!"

The next day, Dr. Mandelík came to pick me up. As soon as we were seated in his black car, he solemnly presented me with a large box of chocolates. I was rather alarmed in case he should expect some mark of favor in return; I was only sixteen and had no experience with men. But he didn't ask for anything. When we went to Podebrady just as he had said, he treated me to tea and cake and we drove home again.

I was only due to stay another five days at Aunt Irma's. He came two more times and drove me around the neighborhood. He talked about his family and his work. On the way home, he laid his hand on my knee. Something twitched inside me and I knew I shouldn't have accepted those chocolates.

When I got home, Father took me aside and gave me some solemn advice.

"You can have everything you want in life," he said. "It's all spread out in front of you, like goods on a table. Just take what you like. But don't forget one thing. As soon as you pick it up, whatever it is, there is a price tag underneath. And that's what you've got to pay."

He looked me straight in the eyes.

"So always weigh up carefully whether what you're so keen on is really worth the cost."

The new school year started. I was in my junior year of high school.

Dr. Mandelík kept sending me long letters to the school, which I bragged about to the other girls, mainly because they had red sealing wax on the back, stamped with the family arms and monogram. He introduced me to the beauties of Czech literature and sent me books of poems: Frána Šrámek's *Stríbrny vítr (Silver Wind)*, Víteslav Nezval's *Sbohem a šátecek (Goodbye and a Scarf)*, and many others. I started to feel important, but not in love. In a detached way it was a flattering adventure, but I never dreamed of anything closer.

There were lightning flashes now from the direction of Germany. Hitler had annexed Austria in March of 1938 and fancied he wanted our Sudetenland region, the militarily significant mountainous area bordering Germany. At various times in history it had been under both German and Czechoslovakian rule. He said it was his by rights and he would take it by force if the Republic didn't cede it voluntarily. We didn't oblige. We mobilized, and the whole nation resolved to stand up against Hitler and his army. Father, like many other patriots, joined up as a volunteer.

Then, in late September 1938, came the Munich Agreement, in which Neville Chamberlain, along with France and Italy, thought they could avoid war by letting Hitler annex the Sudetenland. Czechoslovakia wasn't consulted. No one could believe that England and our other allies had betrayed us, feeding us to a hungry Hitler as a preliminary morsel.

We were caught in a trap. The frontier defenses were laid open, the Germans grabbed the Sudetenland, and our soldiers, Father among them, came home crestfallen. The net tightened around us as the radio blared *Sieg Heil! Sieg Heil!* ever more loudly.

Even so, everyday life proceeded along its well-worn path.

One autumn day, when my parents happened to be in Prague, Dr. Mandelík rang our doorbell. His black Hudson was standing in front of our house. Quite unprepared for such a visit, I was frightened out of my wits. How should I receive him? What should I offer him? How is one supposed to behave when gentlemen like him comes to your home?

He saw my embarrassment and suggested we go to Prague for lunch.

All the way to Prague for lunch? To the world's metropolis? That was a place one only went twice a year, for several days and only after thorough preparation. But to drive there just for lunch? He assured me it was nothing out of the way. So off we went, straight to the Vanha Grill, the most exclusive and fashionable fish restaurant in Prague. It was the first time I'd been there. My knees were trembling, and my hands even more, when the waiter laid out a whole series of forks and variously twisted knives, like surgeon's instruments, on the table in front of me.

To be on the safe side I said I didn't eat fish. But Béra (he wanted me to call him by the name his family used) assured me that they only served the best quality there, and ordered trout and mayonnaise for me. I just about managed to cope without mishap. The room was full of smart company and elegant women. I was anxious either to look like one of them or not be there at all.

After lunch Béra suggested we go to the movies. On the other side of the Wenceslaus Square, Walt Disney's *Snow White and the Seven Dwarfs* was playing—the first ever full-length cartoon film with all the drawings moving and dancing around like live figures. We had never seen anything like it.

When it was over we got into his car and he drove me home as if we had just been around the corner. For Béra it was not extraordinary; but for me the day was like an unforgettable dream.

Winter was setting in and the year would soon be over. Suddenly a bombshell dropped (or so it seemed at the time).

A printed invitation card arrived from Béra, asking me to spend Christmas Eve with him at the family estate in Ratbor. It was a great honor, but what to do? I was a little scared. What preparations should I make? What would I wear? What *did* people wear in those circles?

Mother decided that if a girl was to hold her own and make a proper impression on the Mandelík family, she would have to have a fur coat. She took me to the nearest large town and we went to a furrier. He laid out various samples, including black Persian lamb. Though my opinion wasn't sought, I rejected this on the grounds that I wasn't going to a funeral.

Finally Mother and the furrier settled on a reddish-beige muskrat. Admittedly, this fur was generally used for linings, but they agreed that a coat made from it would look youthful. We went several times for fittings, and finally I could see a three-quarter-length fur coat emerging. Out of the pelts left over the furrier made me a little hat to wear, tipped forward in the fashion of the times. I was looking forward to going out in my new coat right away, but Mother wouldn't hear of it. "This fur coat is to wear on the visit to Ratbor, not out in the street."

So I carried it home in its box and hung it up in the cupboard like a good girl. Mrs. Kuchlerová made me a few more smart dresses as well. In the end I was fitted out like someone going to parade in a fashion show.

There was a peculiar atmosphere now at Aunt Irma's in Kolín. Suddenly they were treating me like an honored guest and admiring my new clothes. They bought me a huge bouquet of flowers to present to Béra's mother on arrival.

Béra picked me up in his car at the appointed time. My aunt's family bade me farewell as solemnly as if I were going to Australia. I sat down in the car with my flowers and agonized about what the evening ahead of me would bring.

Arriving in Ratbor, we first went up a sand-strewn drive through a little park before coming to a halt in front of the mansion. There was an entrance hall with a fountain in the middle and a leather bench running around it. Suddenly Béra was nowhere to be seen. I was faced with a butler who bowed, took from me not only the flowers but my fur coat as well, and went off to put them somewhere. A thought flashed through my mind: I mustn't ever tell Mother that none of the family had ever seen the coat! The way it turned out, I thought, I could just as well have worn it around town or even to school.

The butler came back and led me into the reception room. It was a large, beautiful, furnished drawing room with a Christmas tree in the right hand back corner, all decorated and reaching up to the ceiling.

The room was already crowded with elegant, sophisticated people—a bit on the older side, by my standards—who stood around or sat in various armchairs chatting, some of them sipping drinks from little glasses and generally behaving informally. A good noisy group.

Béra was still nowhere to be seen. Suddenly the butler was back with my flowers in a vase, which he set down in a prominent position.

No one took any notice of me or asked me about anything. There was one little girl playing under the Christmas tree. This was Nina, the daughter of Béra's sister Hana.

Suddenly there was a slight stir as the lady of the house, Mrs. Mandelíková, appeared. She was wearing a dark low-cut dress and her black hair was piled high. She slowly descended the spiral staircase and greeted her guests.

What was I supposed to do? The flowers were in water. How could I give them to her? Yet I had to do it somehow. With one bound I reached the table where they stood, grasped hold of the vase and ran up to the hostess. Mumbling my name or something, I handed her the flowers, vase and all. She was slightly taken aback but said thank you and put them down again on the nearest table.

Everything so far had turned out quite contrary to what I was prepared for.

There was another room adjoining with a large white Bösendorfer piano in it, its lid already open. One of the guests left the others and sat down to play Chopin's Ballade in G minor and, as an encore, the A major Prelude.

When he had finished everyone clapped politely, but I felt that I, as a budding pianist, had appreciated it the most. I knew how accomplished he must be to have played those pieces so well.

After this little concert, which was by way of an interlude, the butler came into the main room with two black-uniformed maids wearing spotless little white aprons and white lace caps and set the scene for Act II. The entire partition wall of the drawing room now rolled back to reveal the dining room, a wondrous sight suggesting not so much a dinner table as a refectory board for twenty-four people with dazzling Yuletide decorations.

In the middle, on a white damask cloth stretching from end to end, was a long pile of Christmas twigs in which stood little colored candle figures, a different figure at each place. One guest had a dwarf, another a toadstool, and so on. There were heavy candlesticks on the table as well, with their own candles. Innumerable cut-glass goblets and silver cutlery glittered in the candlelight.

I was so alarmed to see how many different knives and forks of all shapes and sizes were lying on either side of the pile of plates in front of me, I just couldn't think of food. Béra was sitting opposite me and had no idea of my ignorance and insecurity: I was so afraid of committing some dire faux pas in the course of the evening and ending up as a dreadful failure among all these strange people.

Before the meal started, a telephone rang in the reception room. It was a friend of the family calling from Paris to wish them all a merry Christmas. All that distance: It struck me as the very height of poshness to be rung up from Paris. Anyway, we sat down to eat.

Mrs. Mandelíková sat at one end of the table, with Mr. Mandelík senior, the sugar baron, at the opposite end. Once we were in our places the staff started bringing the food around. There was gleaming white pike with mayonnaise on long silver platters. The butler first offered it to the hostess, who cut off a small slice with a silver knife and put it on her top plate. Then he went around to all the other ladies in strict order according to their personal and family rank, and only afterward started serving the gentlemen. Etiquette was very strict.

One course followed another: fish, soup, roast, poultry with green vegetables and sautéed new potatoes. Finally came chestnut purée with whipped cream and Christmas pastry. Everything was served with various wines. It was these that brought about my downfall. I wasn't used to alcohol but thought it rude to refuse. No one had warned me. After the meal some of the guests withdrew to the smoking room, a cozy little place with brown wooden panels and little red leather armchairs.

Béra invited me to follow him there. My head was already spinning as we went. More drinks were passed round. I'm told that I was very skittish and talked to all the gentlemen; I don't recall that. All I remember is someone offering me a glass of brandy. It was my undoing. The last moments of my visit to the Mandelíks are hazy at best. One of the guests drove me home, apparently, but I can't even remember that. I was gone to the world.

Aunt Irma and her whole family had stayed up to hear my report about the evening in Ratbor, but they couldn't get a word out of me. I dropped straight into bed.

By morning I had sobered up and reality began to dawn. My introduction to the Mandelík family had been a fiasco. Instead of admiration I had earned a bad name. I think I'll keep quiet about all that, I said to myself, and charge it to experience. Next time I won't have anything to drink.

I erased all acquaintance with Dr. Mandelík from my mind. Ah, well, I thought, it hasn't hurt me. Soon I will be home and going back to school. I'll never say a word about it to Mother. She'd only be cross that she had the fur coat made for me for nothing.

I wasn't surprised that Béra didn't even ring up the following day. Just as well; I wouldn't have known what to say. And I didn't want to invent any transparent excuses. Best drop it. It was over. Period.

However, the day before I left Aunt Irma's, Béra did ring, after all, and came to pick me up. I was grateful that he didn't say a word about Christmas Eve. All he wanted to tell me was that he was going to Paris in the new year to work with his uncle for three months. Then he gave me a hug and a goodbye kiss. And so we parted. Though we didn't realize it, both of us were embarking on new stages of our lives.

9. "JÚ ÁR MAJLAKISTA"

Little by little, my life began to be influenced by seemingly far-fetched and quite disconnected events.

Hollywood had released a new film, a musical, *Broadway Melody of 1940*. It included a number of catchy tunes, including "You Are My Lucky Star," which quickly became very popular.

There was not, could not be, the slightest link between me and that film. And yet, life moves in mysterious ways. We were on another of our annual visits to Grandmother's in Prague. Cousin Bedrich was boasting that he had a new phonograph record with songs from the latest films, including *Broadway Melody,* sung by Fred Astaire.

"Let's hear it!" we all cried.

He put the record on the machine and fitted the needle. Fred Astaire's voice filled the room: "You are my lucky star . . ."

Without knowing a word of English, I found the song captivating. Bedrich had to play it for me over and over until I knew it by heart, from start to finish. I had a knack for languages and just as I was able to pick up Rajko's Yugoslav, I could pick up English. I sang it as I heard it, phonetically, with no idea of the meaning. To my ears the opening words sounded like some imaginary Czech words, *Jú ár majlakista,* on the grammatical model of *hokejista,* hockey star, but so what? This is the way it has to sound if it's in English, I decided. And that was that. A thought suddenly came into my mind almost like a premonition as I listened to that song: I had to learn English.

The plan had no practical value at the time. We all spoke Czech at home and school, and I didn't know a soul in England, so what use could the language be to me? Yet an inner voice kept whispering to me that one day I should need it.

When I got back home and started school again, all thoughts of English were forgotten. Meanwhile, the air was full of broadcasts from Germany, Hitler's speeches grew ever more hysterical and threatening, and he now had half his countrymen behind him. Every broadcast by the leader was followed by long-drawn-out chants of *"Sieg Heil! Sieg Heil! Sieg Heil!"* repeated endlessly.

Mother began to feel very anxious, but Father always calmed her down. "Hitler can't do us any harm," he would say. "And if he had the cheek to try, he'd be in for a surprise. We've got a magnificently trained army, strongly fortified frontiers, and a binding treaty of mutual assistance with lots of friendly nations. Keep calm and don't panic."

10. GERMANY INVADES

Father woke us up with a shout. "Quick, children, come to the window, all of you! Right away!"

It was six in the morning. What on earth could be so important as to make Father wake us so early?

There was no brass band coming down the street. Whenever one did, Father always used to join in, picking up a broomstick for a baton and marching around the room like a military band conductor. If anyone was playing "The Radecky March," he could never resist it.

But there was no music this time. It was a miserable winter's day outside, raining with a bit of snow. A day like any other: Wednesday, March 15, 1939.

Father's voice was trembling as he called again. "Come and look out of the window."

We opened the dining room curtains and through the second floor window saw an amazing sight: the German army. It was like a flood rolling down the street. Men on motorcycles, in strange uniforms and iron helmets, were hurtling out of the west in rows and columns, heading toward Prague. It sounded like the roar of an earthquake outside. No one spoke. I felt a chilling premonition of some unknown evil awaiting us.

Forget appeasement and the Sudetenland. Hitler wanted all of Czechoslovakia, and he was taking it.

Apart from the invaders there was not a soul on the street. Only here and there could we see people standing at their windows, gazing with horror at the disaster that was overtaking our nation. There seemed to be no end to the motorized columns; they came in hundreds, perhaps thousands. We rushed to the radio to hear the announcer, with trembling voice, urging the public to keep calm and warning against any form of resistance. Everyone should stay indoors if possible, and the schools would be closed that day.

This was the only good news of the day for me: no school. We were due for an oral geography quiz on the Sahara. I'd done no homework and would have been quite at a loss if I'd been called on. This made me feel a little better.

The radio went on. "Await further announcements."

We squatted around and waited. After about an hour came the nerve racking news that the German army had reached Prague and occupied the presidential Hradcany Castle. It was hard to envision, but everyone realized that this meant the end of the freedom we had known.

Mother was shivering with cold and had to put a warm wrap over her shoulders. Father looked pale. He had never expected this. What changes were to come, how soon, and how they would affect us? There were no answers, only speculation. He was resolved to hold the family together for as long as possible. Next day, we children went back to school and started preparing for the end-of-year exams that would soon be upon us.

Superficially, our lives still seemed unaffected. But a new element was creeping in that we had never known before. Fear. Uncertainty. What would happen next? What would become of us?

The start of the new school year, September 1939, coincided with the German occupation of Poland and the beginning of World War II. Meanwhile, our own Republic had become a Reich Protectorate with a new government, which soon introduced race laws Hitler had been mercilessly applying for years, but which we never believed could be put into place in our country. Yet they were.

Overnight, the entire population was divided into two strictly separate segments—the Jews and the everyone else—as if, at the wave of a wand, we had turned into monsters and subhumans who were to be shunned by everyone else on penalty of imprisonment or worse.

Next came the registration of Jews in every town, village, hamlet, and isolated farm. Each person was given a new identity card stamped *JUDE*. A yellow star had to be sewn on one's jacket so a Jew could be seen from afar and recognized as an enemy.

Immediately after that, the Nazis started registering Jewish property, including businesses, offices, shops, and bank accounts. Every Jewish owner had to surrender his business voluntarily, handing it over, with a signature of consent, to a German proxy and successor. He had to dismiss all his staff, even those with long years of service. Then he had to surrender his domestic pets at collection centers.

Every door began to close. Signs appeared on cafés, restaurants, and cinemas saying *Jews unwelcome.* One well-known shop put up a notice: *Dogs and Jews are not allowed in here.* Ration cards were introduced, with notices that food would only be sold to Jews between three and four o'clock in the afternoon, when there was no more to be had.

More changes came thick and fast, starting with school expulsions. One fine day my father was sent this letter:

BY REGULATION NO. 99761/40–J/1 OF AUG. 7, 1940, THE MINISTRY OF SCHOOLS AND NATIONAL ENLIGHTENMENT, IN AGREEMENT WITH THE REICHSPROTEKTOR, HAS DECREED THAT WITH EFFECT FROM THE BEGINNING OF THE SCHOOL YEAR NO JEWISH PUPILS WILL BE ADMITTED TO CZECH SCHOOLS OF ANY KIND, AND WHERE JEWISH PUPILS HAVE BEEN ATTENDING SUCH SCHOOLS THEY WILL BE EXCLUDED FROM INSTRUCTION FROM THE START OF THE SCHOOL YEAR 1940/41.

I HAVE TO INFORM YOU ACCORDINGLY THAT
YOUR DAUGHTER ZDENKA FANTLOVÁ WILL NO
LONGER BE A PUPIL AT THIS INSTITUTION.
[SIGNED] JAN HORA, HEADMASTER

So my case was settled. As I had finished my junior year, it seemed a shame that I could not complete my last year of school and graduate. My classmates were baffled.

"This is ridiculous. Perhaps it's a mistake. You'll soon see. He'll have second thoughts and you'll find yourselves in school with us."

Ridiculous it certainly was, but it was no mistake. I was never allowed to go back. What now? Where should I turn?

I thought about my options day and night. Suddenly the thought flashed through my mind: learn English! Remember "You Are My Lucky Star"? I'd always wanted to master the language, and now I knew I must. There was an English Institute in Prague where no race laws applied. They took anyone who wanted to learn English. I decided I must go there at all cost.

The first snag was Mother. As soon as I told her I should like to study for another year, learning English at the Institute in Prague, and live at Grandmother's, she turned the idea down flat.

"*You're* not going to stay in Prague. Girls only get corrupted there."

There was no point arguing with her. I saw I had to get around her some other way—by way of my father, in fact. But I needed a well-thought-out plan of action, so he had to say yes. Yes, a year in Prague would be just right.

I'll have to find someone whose opinion he respects, I mused: a teacher. But who? Ah, yes, there was Father's close friend, a former Latin teacher at the high school.

I went to see him. He was rather surprised at my visit but told me to sit down and tell him what was on my mind. I'd carefully prepared what I wanted to say and wasted no time. "I'm sure you'll understand. I've been thrown out of school because of the new race laws. I'm only seventeen and I'm anxious to complete my schooling and take another subject. The English Institute in Prague would surely take me on as a student. It would be no great financial burden on my father to pay the fees for one year. And I have a place where I could stay—my grandmother's on the Old Town Square. Please talk to my father on my behalf. I would so love to have a year at the Institute."

I'm not sure if there were tears in my eyes, but I must have looked very wistful.

He was touched. "You are quite right. A person of your age should spend all the time they can learning and improving themselves. I promise to talk to your father at the first opportunity, and I'll certainly urge him to let you go on with languages."

"Oh, thank you." I sighed and walked home with a light step.

When Father came home the next day he settled down in his armchair, called me in, and made a solemn proposal. "Now what would you think," he started, "about my sending you to the English Institute in Prague for a year so that you could learn another language? You're good at languages, and you can't stay on at the high school."

I answered as casually as I could. "Sounds like a good idea. Why not? I won't be missing out on anything here, and it'll be another foreign language under my belt."

My strategy had paid off. I silently thanked the old Latin teacher once again. Mother never dared to question anything my father suggested, so I went and packed my case. Two days later, Father and I were on our way to Prague.

I felt happy and triumphant. It wasn't just that I was bound for the Institute but something more than that—something mysterious and fateful. I only knew I must learn English. Somehow, sometime, it would be important.

Grandmother still lived in the family house on Tynská Street and the Institute was nearby on the Národní Trída.

I adored my daily walk through the narrow Prague streets, looking at the colorful facades and old family crests on the buildings, trying to imagine how people had lived there over the centuries and what actually went on in the ancient city. Even though I had to wear the yellow Jewish star on my jacket, no one bothered me. I was truly in love with the city. What I most enjoyed was exploring the byways on my own on my way back from the Institute.

Classes were from 9 A.M. to 1 P.M. The teachers were actual Englishmen and Englishwomen, from England. There was a Mr. Henchman, a Miss Hinckley, and others. We had English grammars, read articles from English papers, practiced pronunciation, took dictation and were given homework to do. At a time when there were so few foreigners around, it was like being in contact with a different world.

Up to then, except for the records, I hadn't known or heard a word of the language, but I loved the sound of it, worked hard, and tried to be the best. I looked forward to every class and nothing was too much for me.

Another student my age sat next to me, also from a provincial town, Nepomuk, and also expelled from school on racial grounds. Her name was Marta. We became fast friends, and our destinies seemed to become somehow intertwined.

The two of us used to go on trips outside Prague, once by boat to Zbraslav, another time to Kokorín Castle. We would take the yellow stars off our coats and stride calmly into forbidden areas, going by tram, which was not permitted, and walking home after

8 P.M. when Jewish people were not allowed on the streets. We were confident that no one in Prague would recognize us, and by good luck we were never questioned. Poor Grandmother was scared stiff whenever I failed to arrive before the curfew began.

Marta and I both passed our final exams with distinction. I was particularly proud that my father wouldn't feel he had sent me to the Institute for nothing.

I went to see the old Latin teacher, to show off and to thank him for being the agent of my success. He was pleased and congratulated me. Then in June the academic year ended and I had to go home again, where two events awaited me: one tragic, one happy.

11. FATHER IS ARRESTED

After Prague, life at home seemed very boring, parochial, and empty. The eight o'clock evening curfew was strictly observed, and Stars of David were always worn. They had to be sewn on immaculately, with no loose edges or points. I had to have a needle and thread always ready to make sure the star on every coat was in perfect trim. The German screw was beginning to tighten. People were being arrested for no reason. We couldn't meet anyone, visit anyone, or even stop to talk on the street.

The people of our town quickly became polarized into two camps. There were those who spurned the German regulations and secretly helped us, especially in getting food outside prescribed hours. And there were those who started to collaborate in the hope that the Germans were finally on a winning streak—that *their* time had arrived. These people saw their duty as that of spying on others and denouncing them in return for praise and sundry rewards from the Germans.

I stopped looking up my old friends to avoid causing problems for them and their parents; there were so many new eyes and ears watching and listening. We had always trusted people. We had always been able to talk openly, pass on information, and share ideas without being afraid. But now we were tight-lipped. An ugly monster had crept into our lives: fear of our fellow man. Who could tell if the butcher at the corner, the cigarette vendor opposite (even though he was a disabled World War I veteran), our former washerwoman, or the innkeeper from whom I would fetch my father's beer—anyone—was working with the Germans now, keeping an eye on us, watching for the slightest mistake?

We did not have long to wait. People show their true colors in a crisis.

Under the anti-Semitic regulations we had to hand in our radio and rely on picking up chance fragments of information. One day a neighbor invited my father to come to his home to listen to the news in a Czech-language broadcast from the BBC. Listening to foreign stations was strictly forbidden and subject to grim penalties. Father accepted the invitation and went. He was excited to hear Jan Masaryk, the late president's son, addressing the Czechs and Slovaks from London. My father went to listen exactly twice. Shortly after, when we were sitting around the dinner table at about eight o'clock one evening, the house bell rang—once, twice, three times—followed by a few sharp kicks on the door.

"Gestapo! Aufmachen!" Open up! came the order in German from outside.

My young sister got up and opened the door. Three hefty SS men in uniform burst in, shouting wildly. *"Achtung! Aufstehen!"* "Attention! Stand up!"

We all had to get up from the table. They fell on Father like wild animals. One of them caught him by the collar, shook him, and bellowed, "Name?"

Pale as he was, Father answered calmly, with the German pronunciation of his name, "Ernst Fantl."

"Was?" "What?" the SS man shouted, then told him how he should have answered—Jew Ernst Fantl!—and hit him again.

A scene followed of confused violence and screaming. I was sitting with my back to the wall and had to witness the whole hideous show.

"Jetzt kommst du mit uns!" Now you come with us! the officer in charge added menacingly. Two of the men seized Father by the shoulders while a third prodded and kicked him. Father staggered but managed to straighten up and ask in a quiet voice, "May I take my coat?"

"*Los! Schnell!*" Make haste! One of them went to the bedroom with him. Father emerged with his coat on, holding his hat. Another German was standing astride at the open door in readiness. Father's face was gray, but before leaving the room he turned around to us, looked intensely for a moment at each of us, as if to engrave our features on his memory, and then, in a low but steady voice, said, "Just keep calm. Remember, calmness is strength."

He raised his hat to us in silent farewell.

The Germans slammed the door and Father disappeared into the night.

Mother fainted. When she came to, my brother and sister took her slowly to the bedroom and laid her on the bed.

I sat glued to my chair like a marble statue, incapable of making a move. Once I had recovered from the shock, my eyes fell on the table and the half-eaten meal. Throwing myself wildly at the leftovers, I devoured every scrap on every plate. I needed to get a hold of something to save myself from drowning in the horror, confusion, fear, and loss I had just experienced.

When Mother came back into the dining room and saw what I had done, she scolded me angrily. "How can you eat a single mouthful? It just shows you never loved your father!"

I was too shaken to explain to her that my feelings were not what she thought, quite the opposite.

None of us knew at the time why they had taken Father away, if indeed they had a reason. But we soon found out that a neighbor had informed on him for listening to the BBC broadcast.

We tried in vain to get information as to his whereabouts. Was he merely taken for interrogation from which he might soon return? Or would we never see him again? It took us a long time, with much entreaty and bribing, to discover that he had in fact been taken to the Buchenwald concentration camp. We were allowed to send him a parcel of food, but we never found out whether he got it. There was no communication.

Some months later we received a printed card saying he was in Bayreuth, in Bavaria, in a prison for political offenders and had been given a twelve year sentence for anti-state activity. After that there were short messages from him at long intervals; thus we learned that he was in a labor colony making paper bags—a model inmate who had been appointed leader of his group. I had the feeling that Father, lifelong optimist that he was, had adjusted to conditions and was perhaps a little better off than if he had stayed in Buchenwald, so that gave us some comfort.

Life at home became more and more restricted. We felt like prisoners ourselves, anxiously speculating about what changes might be in store for us. There was really no bright side to look on, and we gradually succumbed to our fate. *Que serà serà.* What will be, will be. We had no choice.

There was one brief moment, before Father was taken away, when Great Britain had offered to accept a limited number of refugees from the Protectorate as domestic servants. I announced at the dinner table that I could apply to this program—go to England and see what happened next. Father turned to me curtly. "Get that out of your head! You're not going anywhere on your own. We are going to stay together, the whole lot of us, just as we are."

And what had happened? We were already minus one.

12. NEW LOVE

Even before the Germans invaded, most of the Jewish families in the Sudeten borderlands had begun to move: some to Prague, some to provincial towns—wherever they had friends or relatives. They were the first to quit their homes out of fear of the Germans, leaving their property and livelihoods behind and relying on whoever might help them. They were generally regarded as second-class citizens. This hardly made for good cheer and optimism. What they didn't realize was that for them, as for all of us, the worst was still to come.

One family that moved into our town were the Levits from Tachov, older parents with a grown-up son, Willi, a barrister, and a younger son, Arnošt, the same name as my father.

Arnošt was a striking young man, a fine physique with soft dark hair and brown eyes that looked straight at you, glowing with courage. He was twenty-three. We met at a neighbor's for tea soon after his family arrived.

One glance and lightning struck—love at first sight and quite inevitable. From that day on we met as often as we could, mostly wandering in the woods, just us two. Arno, as I called him, used to come beneath my window and whistle the melody from Dvořák's *New World* symphony, our signature theme.

I would always drop everything and run outside. I couldn't whistle myself, so when I passed his house I had to ask a passerby to whistle the tune for me. Sometimes they obliged, sometimes they were reluctant—or perhaps they couldn't whistle and didn't want to admit it!

We fell deeply in love, Arno and I, as though we had been waiting for each other all this time. For us, the world turned into a garden of Eden. The German occupation vanished from view. We could see nothing but each other and felt no danger lurking. If there was danger, what of it? Love would overcome all obstacles. A good friend and former schoolmate whom we bumped into on one of our many country walks came up with a suggestion. "Look, I realize you're not supposed to be out after eight, so come to the mill where we live and you can stay with us overnight. Nothing to be afraid of. My people don't take any notice of German regulations anyway."

It sounded tempting but not entirely safe, either for us or for my friend. However, the longing to spend a night together, anywhere, was stronger than our fear of any possible consequences. We settled on Saturday evening. We would go on our bicycles. The mill stood by itself on a stream at the edge of a wood about an hour's walk from town.

But how was I to get out of the house? What would I tell Mother?

I confided the plan to Jiríček. We told Mother only that I and my brother would stay at the mill. My friend would find him some place else to sleep. My brother saw the point and agreed.

We knew exactly what we were getting ourselves into. Without official permission we weren't allowed anywhere outside the town boundaries. There would have been no point in applying for permission. "On what grounds?" they would ask. We had to risk going without permission, which meant we also had to remove the Star of David from our clothes. Both offenses carried heavy penalties, but our minds were made up.

It was a lovely sunny day. Fortune was smiling on us. We put on clothes without the telltale stars. While we were still in town we were scared that someone might recognize us, see that our stars were missing, and report us to the Gestapo. But nobody took any notice of us. Then we were out in the country, where there was very little traffic. We were thinking our difficulties were over, when suddenly an open German army vehicle came around a bend with four uniformed SS men in it. Our breath caught in our throats. Would they stop us? Would they ask who we were and where we were going? Would they ask to see our papers?

We were lucky, guardian angels kept us from danger. The car passed close to us at high speed. Quaking at the knees, we decided to leave the main road and follow a narrow lane between two fields. We knew the way: it would take a bit longer but it would be safer, so we calmed ourselves and proceeded.

Suddenly a German officer appeared, cycling along the lane towards us. He came to a sudden stop, raised his arm and shouted, *"Halt!"*

There was no escape. We thought our end was near. We stopped and jumped off our bikes. I went up to him to speak for the three of us. I looked at him fearlessly in the face, like someone who has nothing to hide.

"How far is it to town from here?" he asked, in a quite normal tone.

Taking a deep breath so my voice wouldn't shake, I said, "If you go this way,"—and pointed—"you can get there in about a half hour. It's not far," I added congenially, as if I were talking to a lost pilgrim.

"Danke." He saluted, and got on his bike, and rode off.

This time we had been really scared and had to sit down by the side of the road to recover our nerves. Finally we reached our destination. The house and the mill stood in a sunny meadow by the forest, and the river bubbled merrily as it passed over the mill wheel. Far and wide not a soul could be seen—like a picture in a storybook—a paradise for lovers. They offered us a small room with a tiny window, with the mill wheel turning just beneath us. There was a straw mattress on the floor, a pillow, and some rough blankets. The moon shone through old wavy windowpanes.

The outside world vanished.

All we had was love, wild, eager, intoxicating, endless. Through the window came the sound of water and the scent of lime trees. Limbs intertwined. If only that night could have gone on forever. We pledged to each other our eternal love and imagined our future together, after the war, as soon as peace came. The next day we rode home, still in a dream.

13. JEWISH TRANSPORTS

In the autumn of 1941, rumors began to circulate that in Prague lists of Jewish families were being drawn up for transportation to the East. Where in the East? No one knew. Reports from relatives in Prague became more unreliable day by day. The name Lodz, a town in Poland, cropped up; apparently a ghetto had been set up there to which transports from our country would be sent. No one was clear whether this was the truth or mere speculation. We were all swathed in uncertainty about the intentions of the Germans.

But there is never smoke without fire, and the stories turned out to be true.

All of a sudden, human transports, a thousand people at a time, were being organized in Prague for dispatch to Poland. Every day we had news of people being summoned and of people who had actually been sent, friends and relatives of ours. Everyone knew it was the beginning of something indescribable, something we had always believed would never happen in our country. Hitler's threats to liquidate the Jewish race in Europe continued to dominate German broadcasts. But as long as you lived at home in your own house and slept in your own bed, you felt safe and "transport" was nothing more than a word. It conjured up no picture. So far it affected only people in Prague, not us in the provinces. Perhaps it would never reach us. Drowning men reach for any straw.

Late one evening our doorbell rang. My brother went to open the door. It was a good friend of my father's, a teacher. He lived near the woods. We let him in and shut the door quickly so that no one would know he had come.

"It's not looking good for you people," he began. "They're already sending transports from Prague to Poland. Your turn is sure to come next; you'll have to leave everything behind. So if you have anything you want to keep safe, pack it up. I'll come tomorrow evening and hide it in our place. Then when the war is over it will be waiting for you. I was very fond of your father, you know."

Good people can always be found, and quite a few were now turning up. Quickly, we put a few pieces together, mainly family photographs, documents, things my mother had been gathering up as dowries for my sister, Lydía, and me: bed linen, monogrammed kitchen towels, tablecloths, and napkins.

We also took down from our dining room wall the painting of Blatná Castle that Father had been so fond of. The place reminded him of his youth and his happy years with his beloved Betty. We added the painting to our little collection. We had no valuables left. Father's business and bank accounts had already been confiscated.

The following day the teacher came as promised and drove away with our things under cover of darkness. The future that awaited us was gradually starting to take shape.

The name Terezín—Theresienstadt to the Germans—the name of a fortress town built during the reign of Emperor Josef II northwest of Prague, meant little to us. Although it was well inside Bohemia, there was seldom occasion to mention this military stronghold. It was under construction for eleven years, between 1780 and 1791, and was surrounded by high walls with small well-fortified entrances.

But suddenly this little town came to the forefront and acquired quite a new reputation. News filtered down that it was being turned into an assembly camp for the Jews of Czechoslovakia. We got out a map and looked to see in which direction Terezín lay from Prague. It didn't seem so horrible. If they deported us there, we pondered, we would still be on our home territory, still more or less at home—just elsewhere, in a different town.

We didn't have long to wait before the first two transports were sent from Prague. They were called AK1 and AK2—AK for *Arbeitskommando,* labor detachment—and consisted of 2,000 young men. Their assignment was to carry out construction work that would prepare Terezín to accommodate the many Jews who were going to be sent there. That was in November 1941.

This development struck at the heart of our family. My cousin Bedrich, the one who had introduced me to Fred Astaire's version of "You Are My Lucky Star," was sent away on the first transport. He was only sixteen. His parents tore out their hair over his untimely departure. He was an only child, pampered by his family. He had always had everything he wanted and showed little appreciation.

Everyone thought he would come to no good, but fate works in strange ways with some people. He turned into a warrior overnight: strong, brave, and fearless. His parents thought they would never see him again; but they did, albeit briefly, ten months later, when they were reunited in Terezín.

The whispers and rumors were becoming reality before our eyes. Gradually we accepted the fact that there was no escape from the Germans and their plans for us, and we had to resign ourselves to everything that lay in store. Our prayers, Arno's and mine, were simply that we would not be sent on separate transports. If God loved us he would let us go together, inseparable, wherever we were sent. As long as we were together, nothing bad could happen to us.

Our turn did come, sooner than we had thought. At the beginning of January 1942, we were summoned to a large nearby town to be registered. This took place in the main hall of the district office. There was a large crowd assembled from a wide area of towns, villages, and isolated farms. We stood in rows facing uniformed Germans behind a table. Each of us stepped forward, gave his name and address, and was given a narrow slip of paper with a transport number.

My heart was pounding with fear—not about where I would be sent but lest Arno would be sent somewhere else. He and his family were in a row in front of me and already had their registration slips. Their transport had the letter R. I was trembling to know what mine would be. It was like a roulette game. Nobody had the faintest idea what would turn up.

We were out of luck. My family and I were assigned to transport S. My worst fears were borne out; Arno and I would be separated. In my despair I felt like falling on my knees and begging the SS men to let us go together. But I knew that pleading would be worse than useless. The crowd was tense and noisy and the Germans had started shouting *"Aufgehen! Aufgehen!"*—Keep Moving!—to try and speed things up. "Let's be finished with you!" Blows fell even at this stage.

Suddenly I noticed amidst the confusion that my mother—she was the first of us to be called—had S 204 on her slip, my brother S 205, and my sister S 206. Mine was S 716! I felt as if an icy hand of destiny had touched me. What could this mean? I would be leaving on the same transport, but at some point fate would separate us. Was this a good or a bad sign? In my misery I decided it must be bad. I was so apprehensive. In that room, in the space of a few hours, they had turned us into numbers and wreaked havoc in our lives. I was prepared to go to the very depths of hell with Arno, but now I was on my own, cut off from him and from my own family as well.

Transport R was scheduled to leave on January 16, 1942, destination unknown. The Germans never revealed anything in advance. Perhaps it was bound for Terezín, perhaps elsewhere. I was distraught. Arno was leaving me. Why did our love have to be so short lived? Perhaps God in heaven would take pity on us and send us to the same place. I grasped at the faintest hope and persuaded myself that all was not yet lost. I sat with his family until they were taken away, rolling up Arno's socks and putting them in his suitcase. I took the chain and four-leaf clover charm I wore round my neck and put it in his hand. "Here, take this for luck."

The next morning he was gone.

The S transport was scheduled to leave four days later, on January 20. There was no time for lamentation. We were leaving home and we had to get everything ready. Each person was allowed to take one suitcase and a bedroll: a pillow, a sheet, and, if possible, a blanket that would be rolled up in a canvas bag with the transport number sewn onto it. The suitcase also had to be carefully labeled with our name and transport number painted white, indelibly, across the front in large letters.

The next question was what to put in the suitcase. Clothes? Food? For how long? Winter things? Summer things? Everyone's advice was different. One well-meaning neighbor slipped through our door and counseled us earnestly. "The most important thing to take is boots, warm comfortable ones. Suppose you are forced to march somewhere? Then warm underclothing. And gloves. Woolly caps. Hands, feet, and head have to be kept warm."

Someone else said it was more important to take food: bread, tins of fat drippings, and so forth. Our former shop assistant Matysek (as Father called him after his fifteen years of service) also came to tell us what he had learned though the grapevine: "Forget about food and clothing. What you must have is a supply of soap and, above all, cigarettes. Cigarettes are the most valuable currency in those places. You can get whatever you want with them. I have this from someone who knows the local police on duty around Terezín. They can't be wrong." He stood by this advice, and in fact he was quite right. Cigarettes were indeed the top currency. Soap was already rationed and hard to come by. In any case, it was poor sandy stuff and always in short supply.

We packed a bit of everything in our cases. Warm clothing, a few tins of food, soap cubes, and, if there was still room, a supply of that highly rated wartime commodity, cigarettes.

Finally, we meticulously tidied up the house, leaving everything shipshape as if we were going off on a summer holiday and wanted things to be orderly when we got back. I sat down at the piano for the last time and played two pieces that seemed to convey a sense of hope, Dvořák's Waltz in D flat major and Sinding's "Rustle of Spring". Then I stroked the keys goodbye and closed the lid. I even locked it, so that nothing untoward would happen to it before we met again.

14. OUR TIME HAD COME

Early the next morning we got ready to leave. It was Tuesday, January 20, 1942, a beautiful winter day with a cloudless sky. The temperature was well below freezing, frost was on the trees, and the cold stung your nose—the sort of day that, at another time, would make you glad to be alive. We loaded our cases and other baggage onto a two-wheeled pushcart and set off for the railway station. My brother and I pulled the cart while my mother and sister walked behind it with heads bowed liked bereaved relatives at a funeral. People who met us either looked aside or slipped quickly into doorways to hide their true thoughts. Did they feel sympathy or loathing? A few actually shouted words of encouragement, like, "Don't worry! You'll soon be back."

Others came up to us quietly, muttering, "It's your turn now. It'll be ours next."

On the way, I ran into my best friend, Vera. She wore woolen stockings, a bright warm sweater, red knitted cap, and gloves to match. She was carrying her clip-on ice skates in one hand and the fastening key in the other. She stopped.

"Where are you off to?" she asked.

"Don't really know. They haven't told us. Some concentration camp, I expect."

"Ah, that's silly. There was a deep frost overnight, down to minus fifteen, I think. The ice'll be strong today. Pity you can't come. Perhaps you'll be back before the winter's over. The water's sure to stay frozen for a long time. Cheerio, then!"

"Cheerio!"

So Vera went off to skate, and I went . . . who could say where?

. . .

In the big town nearby, a train was standing ready on the siding with a large crowd of people milling around it. Young, old, mothers with children. All around them on the ground lay their luggage with their names and transport numbers painted in white. The whole group was surrounded by uniformed SS men. Some of them were holding dogs by the leash, others were going around shouting orders and pushing people into the cars.

"*Alle einsteigen!*" "Everyone get in! Right away—faster, faster!"

Everything was in confusion. Children were screaming and mothers were trying to quiet them down, though they were just as scared themselves. Some elderly people were too weak to climb in quickly so blows rained down.

Father's words rang in my ears: "Just keep calm. Remember, calmness is strength." I wondered where he was now. The thought struck me that even if he could write a letter we would never get it. And he would never find out where we were sent.

It's everyone for himself now—to the best of his ability.

And what about Arno? How would it all end? Would we ever see each other again? Life had suddenly become one big question mark.

Crammed full of people and luggage, the train finally moved off. Before it did, every compartment was securely locked and brown-uniformed Schutzpolizei, police guards, all drunk, were ordered to keep watch over us. They carried short whips with lead balls on the end and patrolled the train continuously, from coach to coach. There were a lot of them. As soon as they came into a coach they yelled out "*Achtung!*" and everyone had to get up and stand at attention. If anyone was asleep he was whipped across the face. Woe to anyone who was not clean-shaven, they would shave off his beard with a dry razor until the skin bled. If there was no blood, there was no fun in it. I gradually grew accustomed to, though never reconciled with, German brutality and sadism.

Outside the train the same gently rolling landscape flashed by: familiar fields with a crow pecking in a furrow here and there, the silent trees alongside the snow-covered tracks—the same scene as when we rode along that very stretch to visit Grandmother in Prague. How I had always enjoyed watching at the window and looking forward to getting off at the Wilson Central Station where everyone would welcome us.

Now here we were, prisoners in locked coaches. This time it was the landscape outside, silent and sad, looking in at us.

. . .

Our train stopped on sidings from time to time. It took two days and two nights for us to reach our destination, Terezín. I was impatient to get out. For me, Terezín meant that Arno was already there, waiting for me as eagerly as I for him. Any moment now our eyes would meet and we would fall into each other's arms. Just be patient. Terezín was the place of my prayers. The place where I most yearned to go. God would be kind to us after all. Arno was my life. I longed to be with him again. Hunger, cold, and fear of the Germans—these held no terror for me. Nothing was as frightening as never being with Arno again.

Etched in front of our eyes at last were the walls of Terezín. In the middle of the city gate was the green uniform of a Czech gendarme. We did not have to worry about finding ourselves in some unknown place in a foreign country. We were still on the territory of our Czechoslovak Republic, and that was some comfort. The gendarmes were talking Czech, which seemed a good sign. They escorted us through the interior of the town, its square street grid lined with low houses.

The dominant feature, however, was a group of about ten huge barracks, three or four stories high, enclosing large courtyards. At each level, on all four sides of the courtyard, there was a long gallery from corner to corner. Until then Terezín had been a town where garrisons were quartered in the barracks and civilians lived in the houses. Just before our arrival the army had been moved out, but the civilian population of about 5,000 remained.

Each barracks had a German name, of some German city or region. Thus there was now a Dresden barracks (Dresden for short), Hamburg, Magdeburg, Hannover, Sudetenkaserne, Hohenelbe (Vrchlabí for us Czechs), Kavalier (Kavalírka), and so on.

Each building acquired a new character according to its inmates. Sudeten and Hannover were men's quarters. Dresden and Hamburg were only for women. Magdeburg became the center of activities; it housed the Terezín administrative center and the Jewish Council of Elders. In a building on the town square was the German *Kommandantura*, the German High Command Headquarters.

Our transport was quickly split up into men and women with children.

All the men were allocated to Sudeten while we women went to Hamburg. Our family was now split up: my brother went off with the other men and we three women prepared to move into the women's quarters. For the moment, we stood in the courtyard with our baggage, waiting to have rooms, or billets, assigned to us. These billets were entered from the long galleries around the courtyards. Each contained three-tier bunks put up by the boys from the first work details, the *Arbeitskommando*. The bunks were designed according to our new living space allowance: twenty-seven square feet per person. Bunks were separated by narrow aisles. Each little billet was equipped with at least four or five bunks, thus providing for twelve to fifteen people.

We were prepared for what the Germans in the train had promised us—to sleep on concrete or outside in the frost—but instead we had our own bed in a room with a roof overhead, sheltered from rain and wind, where you could stretch out and sleep under your own blanket. It seemed a luxury, even if your living space was very small.

Our billet was on the third floor and we were lucky to be given a bunk by a window. We divided our family premises up so that Mother was sleeping on the bottom tier, my sister on the middle, and I on the top with a small ladder attached to it. We stuffed the suitcases under Mother's bed, put some coathooks in the wall, and laid out our utensils and dishes on the windowsill. And there we were, settled in our new "flat."

As per our instructions we elected a *Zimmerälteste*, or room leader, who had to see that the billet was tidy and that peace and quiet prevailed among the inmates. Her most important job was to divide up the bread ration twice a week. As long as we still had supplies of food brought from home, we were very happy to get our third of a loaf each time. But once our food ran out, we eyed each portion critically in terms of size and our fair share.

We had to accustom ourselves very quickly to living in such close quarters—one room—with other people. We were all in the same situation, but everyone reacted differently. Older women became depressed and intolerant, complaining about things incessantly. We younger ones took it more in stride, as if we were sleeping under canvas in a girl scout summer camp. Suddenly we found ourselves thrown together with new people, and we began to form new friendships.

15. LOVE IN A STORAGE BIN

My main concern was when and where to meet Arno. Each barracks with its new complement of civilians was sealed off, and no one could get out. Although I had found out that Arno was quartered in a building just around the corner, he was as far away from me as if he were on another planet. I started to fret. I had been there a week and still we had had no contact. Suppose they sent him off somewhere else, "farther east," as the phrase went, and we never saw each other again? Life began to seem absurd, yet the thought that he was sleeping only a short distance away, thinking about me as I was about him, warmed my heart. I was sure he would find an opportunity to get out of his barracks. I didn't have to wait long. The rumor spread through our galleries one day that a new supply of potatoes had reached the barracks, destined for the communal kitchen. As I ran out of our billet I could hear the crescendo of our signature Dvořák tune being whistled, sweet and clear.

It had to be Arno! I ran over to the low gallery wall with such a rush that I almost fell down into the courtyard from the third floor. There he was, standing with six other men next to a cartload of potatoes. He had his belted winter coat on and was looking around to find me. I ran down the staircase as if it were a playground slide and our eyes met. Meanwhile, someone was organizing a squad of twenty women to peel potatoes. I immediately volunteered and, luckily, was included. The rest had to go back into their billets. Arno was with the men unloading the potatoes.

Only a few yards separated us. We were desperately longing to be together. But how? And where?

Amid the commotion in the yard, we managed to get away from the others and run into a gallery where there were stairs. We followed the stairs down and found ourselves in a cellar lined with empty storage bins. Each bin had a heavy iron door. We had so little time, and our desire was urgent.

Throwing ourselves at the first door, we found it locked tight. The same with the door next to it. Desperately we pushed at a third door, blinded by ardor and oblivious to danger. The door opened, creaking just a little. Huddled in a dark corner behind the door we kissed with insane passion—and all the rest. The barracks seemed to vanish along with the Germans, Terezín, and the world itself. Here, together, one soul, one body alone in the universe. I cannot say how long it lasted.

Suddenly, we heard footsteps in the corridor outside, heavy, regular, military ones. No question about it: a German patrol. By the sound, there must be three men, and now we could also hear their voices. We knew this was it. They would be bound to find us; the penalty was death. I could only pray that we would not be tortured as well.

They unlocked the first door and looked inside. Then the second one next to ours. We stood pressed to the wall, clinched together. If they were going to check every bin methodically, ours was next. They stopped in front of our door, pressed down the handle, and evidently wondered why the door was not locked like the others.

"*Was ist da los?*" What's up with this one?

One of the Germans pushed it open with a jerk. The door banged against the wall beside us. One SS man planted himself in front of the doorway. We could see the soles of his boots. We held our breath. Only the thickness of the door panel stood between us and certain death.

"*Mach doch mal Licht,*" the commander ordered. Let's have some light.

Our hearts stopped as they switched on powerful flashlights that lit up the whole bin. For what seemed like an eternity the beams traveled over the walls and the floor. I struggled not to make a sound, even though the dust was beginning to irritate my nose. . . .

"*Weiter gehen!*" Next!

The order to proceed rang out. Finding nothing, they switched off their flashlights and left, slamming the door behind them.

Supposing they had locked us in—what would become of us? But they didn't.

It was some time before we came to our senses. As soon as the sound of their footsteps had died away we ran upstairs into the courtyard, where the potatoes were now all unloaded. I quickly returned to my place among the potato peelers, while Arno joined his squad, which was just leaving. We exchanged a quick look in silent farewell. We knew it would be a while before we saw each other again, but the memory of our lovemaking would keep our hearts warm.

More and more transports from Prague and other Czech cities kept pouring into Terezín. Among the newcomers were friends and relatives whom we had been prevented from visiting because of the new race laws. Now, here we were, all together. Even Grandmother turned up. We managed to get her into our billet. With the help of our supply of cigarettes we changed bunks so she could move right next to us in our corner. Mother was happy to have her near and did all she could to look after her.

Terezín was filling up so rapidly that the 5,000 original inhabitants had to be moved out on short notice. It really looked as if this place was meant as a permanent colony for all the Jews of Bohemia and Moravia. There was even a slight relaxation of the rules on movement between male and female barracks, and it became possible to get an exit pass to various grounds.

Arno always managed to find a pretext. His so-called forwarding detachment had more freedom of movement than others. It was they who brought in food supplies and distributed them from barracks to barracks, so he often turned up at Hamburg. He only had to whistle our tune, and we had a chance to see each other and exchange news, however briefly. I had a permanent place with the potato squad. The peelings were carted off to German farmers in the surrounding countryside, who fed them to their pigs, but I always managed to sneak a few into our billet for Mother to make hot soup on our small stove.

The bodies in our overcrowded rooms and bunks attracted fleas and bedbugs. They multiplied fast and crawled up the walls, where they were swatted and left red stains behind. When we ate they would sometimes fall into our soup. We scooped them out gingerly with the tip of a spoon, so as to waste as little soup as possible, flicked them on to the floor, squashed them, and went on eating.

In March, Arno unexpectedly appeared one day with a birthday present for me: a small folding stool he had made out of bits of wood. We fitted it into our family corner, and now we could say we had some furniture. Anyone who wished could sit on it, but I got the most enjoyment from it and carved his name on it.

As winter slowly gave way to spring, hopes rose that we might be home again by summertime. But the reality was quite different. Not only did more and more transports arrive, but more and more left as well.

Where to was a secret. "To the East" was all we were told. So everyone dreaded them, though no one knew what awaited there. No one had ever returned, no reports ever reached us. The very word East acquired a sinister meaning. There was no predictable pattern. One day there would be a transport composed of whole families. The next would consist only of people over sixty-five, or only of young men fit for hard labor. No one had any reliable information. It was all fear and speculation. But as long as we remained in Terezín we seemed to enjoy relative safety. We felt almost at home.

The central registration office in Magdeburg, where the Jewish self-administration Council of Elders operated, worked in shifts around the clock. As people arrived and departed, each name had to be recorded, along with the person's age and transport number. If you were unlucky you got a narrow pink slip with your name and transport number on it and had to present yourself within twenty-four hours at the train waiting on the siding. There you got into a cattle car, which the Germans locked and sealed, and the train moved off into the unknown with its human cargo.

This was the fate that befell Arno and his family one day in June 1942. He came to tell me, flouting the risk of being caught. He felt he now had nothing more to lose. All he could say was, "We've been put on a penal transport. It's a reprisal for the killing of Heydrich." We all knew the senior German official in Prague, Reichsprotektor Reinhard Heydrich, had been assassinated.

I was dumbstruck.

His transport of 2,000 people was to leave the following day. I awoke at four that morning. Arno was standing on the ladder to my bunk, wearing his gray belted coat and all ready to go. I had no idea how he had managed to get into our barracks at that time of night. He was breathless with excitement. He took my hand, slipped a little tin ring over my finger, and said, "That's for our engagement. And to keep you safe. If we're both alive when the war ends, I'll find you."

He embraced me, kissed me, and jumped down. Closing the door quietly behind him, he was gone. At five o'clock he left with the rest of his transport.

On the inside of his homemade tin ring he had engraved *Arno 13.6.1942.*

Once Arno had gone, Terezín was a wasteland for me. There was no one to whistle Dvořák, nothing and nobody to look forward to. Arno and his entire transport vanished as if the earth had swallowed them up. There were no rumors as to where they might have been taken—not the slightest scrap of information. What was the difference between an everyday transport "to the East" and a "penal transport"? No one had an answer.

I felt sure that, with all his courage and resourcefulness, Arno would manage to adapt himself and find the strength to survive all the hardships and cruelty that lay in wait. The war was sure to end soon, and then we would somehow find each other. I had his ring on my finger. It bound us together, whatever the distance that separated us.

There was no time for tears and personal woes. A collective tragedy had descended on us all, like some natural disaster that forces people together. All that remained was hope and the determination to survive. People continued to say goodbye to each other and wish each other a safe journey and a happy return. We all trusted that this storm of rage and madness would one day blow over and we would all come together again, return to our homes, and start new lives.

Spring was well on its way now, but none of us had yet returned home as our neighbors had predicted when we left. The ice on the skating pond must have long since melted, and Vera would have put her skates away in the cupboard for next winter. There would be willows and lamb's tails in the bushes all around. Would I ever see them again? We lived in a different world these days, where nothing grew and nothing blossomed. There was no green grass, just the massive, cheerless barracks walls. The memory of our moment of love—Arno's and mine—soon after our arrival was all that kept my heart warm.

16. LIFE IN TEREZÍN

The evacuation of the original Terezín inhabitants had to be speeded up as fresh transports of thousands of people flooded in—now not only from Bohemia but also from German cities such as Aachen, Cologne, and Berlin. The new arrivals from Germany were mainly elderly people with masses of luggage. They had been told they were being taken to spas where they would lack for nothing, medically or socially, so many of them had packed dinner suits and evening dresses with long gloves and the feather hats that were then in fashion.

On arrival, their luggage was loaded onto long-shafted black funeral carts with fancy carvings. Under normal circumstances they would have been pulled by horses, but at Terezín they were pulled by ten boys from a forward detachment. These four-wheeled carts were the only means of conveyance available in the town, and were used for transporting all manner of things: cases, loaves from the baker, groceries, and sometimes old people from the incoming transports who were too weak to walk. On other occasions they served their traditional purpose, carrying corpses to the crematorium. Terezín wasn't an extermination camp, but with disease, malnutrition, and so many elderly, the crematorium was kept busy.

Transports came, transports went; no sooner had people exchanged welcome greetings than they were parting again, saying goodbye. Everywhere it was very busy; the town never paused for breath. On the contrary, once the 5,000 original inhabitants had been moved out, new ones came in until the population totaled nearly 60,000.

Every free space had to be utilized for living quarters. Not only the barracks but all the surrounding houses and even shop windows were used for accommodation, with three-tiered bunks installed everywhere for living and sleeping. All the barracks gates were opened now, and we were able to move freely about the town and visit one another. It really seemed as if things were looking up. Only Arno was missing. How happy we would have been now.

One day a Prague transport arrived with Bedrich's parents and grandmother. There were tears of happiness. They had brought supplies of fresh food with them. We had a great party to celebrate our lucky reunion, just as we used to have in their Prague home. Life seemed not so terrible after all. But our gaiety was short-lived. Just ten days went by before Bedrich's father, mother, and grandmother were summoned to join the next transport to the East. The joy of our reunion was replaced with separation, sadness, and tears.

For the time being, Bedrich himself stayed on with us. Apparently the authorities were not including healthy young men in the transports; they were needed to keep the town and all its services functioning. Every able-bodied person was now mobilized. Terezín was turned into a little autonomous state of its own, run by its Council of Elders with their own triumvirate.

The three elders were academics from three different universities—in Prague, Berlin, and Vienna. They all had similar names: Dr. Edelstein, Dr. Epstein and Dr. Murmelstein. This strange trio was picked by the Germans to secure the smooth and efficient running of all communal affairs, but also to decide the composition of transports to the East, a thousand people at a time—against their will, against their conscience.

We scarcely saw any Germans on the streets. They all sat in their large headquarters, from where they issued orders, punished offenses, and dispatched people—to somewhere.

We never knew what happened to them.

. . .

To feed 60,000 people three times a day, however inadequately, was no small task. Huge kitchens were set up in the cellars of all the big barracks, each to cook for 6,000.

I was now promoted from potato peeler to kitchen duty in Hannover. It looked less like a kitchen than a major industrial production unit. Great fifty-liter boilers were installed close together along three sides of the area and heated from underneath. To be a kitchen stoker was a superior and much sought-after job.

In front of each boiler was a wooden step on which we stood to stir whatever was cooking inside. There were no choice ingredients. Morning and evening we made "coffee," a warm brown concoction, a coffee substitute. At noon there was "food." Once or twice a week this featured a slice of horse meat with a little brown cube of gravy, plus one potato. Sometimes the horse meat was served as "goulash."

Once a week there was a yeast dumpling with "chocolate" sauce, a brown liquid made from a synthetic powder with artificial sweetener. Sometimes there was just a watery soup with a slice of parsnip and a piece of potato floating in it. In the evening was the "coffee" again.

We worked around the clock in the three shifts. The first shift was from 2 A.M. to 10 A.M.; the second from 10 A.M. to 6 P.M. in the evening; and the third from 6 P.M. to 2 A.M. again. Each group was comprised of fifteen to twenty people—men and women mixed—under a leader, the *parták*, as we Czech-speakers called him. We were issued rubber boots because the concrete floor was always wet, having to be continually swept and hosed down. Cleanliness had to be maintained, but there was no avoiding untoward incidents. There were pipes running along the walls, as is normal in basements. On one night shift when "goulash" was being cooked, a large gray rat was seen scurrying along the pipe.

There was a great commotion. The girls screamed, but the boys were merciless. The rat stopped to look around. One of the boys egged on his friend next to him, "Why don't you take that shovel, Otouš, and knock him off into the boiler!"

Without hesitation, Otouš swung the shovel and felled the animal into the goulash. Everyone was delighted. "We got it!"

When the *parták* saw what had happened he bellowed, "Fish it out right away and don't breath a word to anybody!"

Otouš, however, feeling he deserved credit for successfully disposing of the rat, wouldn't have it. "Oh, why not leave it in? At least there will be more meat."

One WIPO guard (short for Wirtschaftspolizei, or "household police") was assigned to each kitchen to ensure that no food was stolen. Rations reached the kitchen in quantities precisely calculated on a scale fixed by the Germans. The WIPO were the inmates' own inspectors and were responsible for any loss or theft, for which there were severe penalties. But for the most part we all behaved impeccably, and everything went as it should.

There was an eight o'clock curfew in the town, which was strictly observed. Anyone caught on the street after that was punished. Only those who needed to move about to perform their various duties had after hours passes, and all of us who worked the night shift in the kitchens had passes in case we were stopped by a patrol.

The streets at night were empty and unlighted. I always carried a Dynamo flashlight in my pocket, along with my pass. This was a great treasure that I had brought with me from home. It looked like a little gray mouse, fit neatly in my palm, and lit up if you rhythmically squeezed a little metal lever. As I went along in the darkness, it kept on whistling to itself—*ooh-eee, ooh-eee*—and I had the feeling of not being alone.

Walking around Terezín at night, you might think you were in a haven of peace and safety—not a sound, no sign of life. You couldn't tell there were 60,000 weary, hungry souls there, spending restless nights in their two and a half square meters of living space, awaiting their fate.

No cat or dog ever ran across the street.

Food was distributed regularly three times a day. A large container of soup was placed in a recess in the kitchen, filled with an exact number of helpings. We stood behind the soup with a ladle in hand. In front of this recess stood a duty officer of the *Menagedienst*, a ticket controller, equipped with a little punch for making a hole in the meal coupon that everyone had to produce when they received their food. It was like having your ticket punched by a train conductor.

Before any food appeared in the recess, a long line of people waited patiently with their mess tins and spoons. The majority were old people, who stood very still, huddled together, silent and hungry. One could see from their expressions that the one ladle of soup meant the chance to survive perhaps one more day. It was a sad job serving them. An old man would come up, hold out his tin with trembling hands, and mutter imploringly, *"Von unten, bitte, Fräulein"*—from the bottom, please, miss. There was always the hope that a ladle scraping the bottom might bring up a piece of potato or cabbage that would make their day, as if they had won the lottery. We always tried to be helpful.

Of those sick or elderly men and women condemned to spend the rest of their lives here, about two hundred died every day. And more and more of them were now arriving through an endless revolving door. Off a transport and into Terezín, then back onto a transport for the journey east.

. . .

One day Marta, my friend from the English Institute, turned up on a Prague transport. We hugged each other like long-lost sisters. Marta had married Karel Bloch, a wonderful doctor who suffered from tuberculosis. She was quick to introduce me to her husband, a haggard man with twinkling eyes. There was no tragedy in his appearance, and Marta was obviously happy.

They were both assigned to the medical staff: Karel as a doctor and Marta as a nurse, both entitled to wear a uniform. They were not billeted together, but we all often met when our shifts allowed, sitting in her room or on my bunk, chatting endlessly. It was lovely to be together. We did not miss the ambiance of a smart café or posh flat with soft armchairs; we simply were together. That was the main thing.

Around that time, the Accommodation Department started allocating small spaces in the extensive attics to some of the more distinguished inmates to create "penthouses" for themselves. A penthouse was meant for married couples, and there were many applicants. The lucky ones either had contacts in high circles or simply paid for their penthouse as on any black market.

Soon after penthouses started proliferating, dormer windows with curtains began to appear on every roof. Some people seemed to be settling down as if they expected to stay for good.

Here and there the end of a long corridor was fenced off with a wooden partition, giving rise to a *kumbál,* a cubby hole just for one person. I applied for one of them on the grounds of my irregular working hours and the difficulty of sleeping during the day in a billet with so many people around. I had a few good friends in high places who helped me, and I was given a cubby with a window, at the end of a long corridor in a former private home. My friends in the carpentry shop made a wooden partition, a door with a lock, a few shelves on the wall, a folding table, and a cupboard in the corner for my clothes. I had a bedstead, a mattress, and a small stove under the window for heat in the winter. My new room was reminiscent of a sleeping compartment on a night train—an absolute luxury for one person. Just opposite me in another cubby lived a well known Prague nightclub musician, Wolfi Lederer, and his wife. I had good neighbors.

But I had barely settled in when I suddenly found myself in mortal danger.

17. MARTA AND HER UNIFORM

One day news got around that a transport was leaving for the East in two days time, comprised entirely of the sick and elderly.

No one I knew was on the list, so I went calmly on with my work. The following day at about ten o'clock in the evening I saw from my window two boys with a stretcher coming into my building. I assumed they were picking up some elderly person designated for transport and settled back in bed with a book.

Moments later came a knock on my own door. I opened up, and there were the two young men with the stretcher. They must have failed to find the person they're looking for, I thought, and have come to ask where she lives. Not at all. They had a slip with my name on it: Fantlová Zdenka.

"Is this you?" they asked.

The situation struck me as ridiculous. "Yes, that's my name," I said dismissively, "but there must be some mistake. As you can see, I'm neither ill nor elderly, after all."

They took another look at the slip. "This is your name clear enough, so we'll have to follow orders and take you along to the Podmokly sluice." That was the collecting point for those about to be transported.

My brain worked fast. *If they carry me off on this stretcher I'm done for,* I thought. *I mustn't on any account leave my cubby.* It struck me that I had a good friend Pavel, who was on duty that night at the central registry in the administrative building. He would know what had happened and help in some way to get me off the transport list.

There was no time to hesitate. The young porters stood over me with their stretcher propped against the wall. I grabbed pencil and paper and wrote, *My name's on the transport list and they've come to take me to the sluice. Tell me what to do.* I folded the paper, wrote Pavel's name on it, and gave one of the lads one of my last three cigarettes to take it to the Magdeburg Barracks, find Pavel, and come back with an answer. It took a little while. All kinds of thoughts were racing through my head.

Surely I couldn't just go off on my own without telling anyone. Not even my Mother would know I had suddenly disappeared. That can't be possible, I argued. But in my heart I knew here anything was possible. A half hour later the young man returned with Pavel's answer, but it was not what I expected.

Let them carry you away. Leave the rest to me.

There was nothing else for me to do. I felt sure I would be back very soon and had no need to dress for anything. So they carted me off just as I was, in my nightdress with a blanket thrown over me. It was about eleven o'clock when we arrived at the Podmokly sluice on the edge of the town, behind which was a siding where a transport train stood ready.

We went down a long drive lined with uniformed SS men on either side, checking the new arrivals. One of them had a list from which he crossed off the name of the person on each stretcher. The reception panel included two Jewish doctors, officially nominated. The situation looked bad. I knew full well that no one who entered the collection center ever got out. If anyone tried to escape from a transport he was sure to be caught and end up in the *Kleine Festung,* the Little Fortress in the Terezín tower, to be shot or hanged. Several people had already met their end there.

The porters carried me up a wooden staircase to the second floor where the collection center was located. It was a huge bare room full of people lying on stretchers, one beside another. I shut my eyes.

An official kept shouting out names, and whoever answered was quickly carried away. After about a half hour I heard my name called: "Fantlová Zdenka!"

I remained silent—not a word—and kept my eyes shut. I mustn't answer at any cost. Perhaps there was still a chance that my friend would work some miracle to save me. Time passed. They kept bringing in more and more people. But a great number had also been taken away.

"Fantlová Zdenka!" Again I heard my name being called out. My heart was pounding. Supposing Pavel, with the best intentions in the world, had not managed to get me off the list? I would be taken away with all these sick old people in my nightdress and one blanket.

I began to get really scared. The clock on the wall said 2 A.M.

At that moment Pavel came into the room. My eyes gleamed at the sight of an angel arriving to save me. But he hadn't.

"Zdenka," he said miserably, "It looks bad. There's no chance of getting you off the list at this point. But perhaps something can be done. Dr. Skalsky will be coming along in a moment and may be able to dream something up. Meanwhile, don't answer if they call your name."

I started to realize how grim the situation was.

Dr. Pepík Skalsky was a fair-haired young man of farming stock from our own part of the countryside. He had been a good friend of my brother. I waited impatiently for him, as the ranks of stretcher cases began to thin out.

"Fantlová Zdenka!" The official was now calling my name at shorter intervals. *As long as I stay silent I've got a chance,* I told myself, and kept my eyes fixed on the door. Suddenly I saw Pepík coming in. I motioned to alert him to where I was. He knelt down next to me and said very seriously, "The only way to get you off the transport now is if I give you an injection of milk. You'll get a high temperature, and they don't take people with fever. Don't answer to your name yet. I'll come back in a moment with everything necessary." He hurried out.

"Fantlová Zdenka!" There was my name again. The official looked all around the now half-empty room. Time dragged on inexorably. I must not, must not answer. No one here knows who I am, and even if I have to go, I must be the last one.

After a half hour, Pepík was back again. Being a doctor he could come and go as he pleased. And amid all the uncertainties of Terezín there was one thing we could be sure of: We always helped one another to the best of our abilities, even in the dead of night. Everyone did his best for a friend.

He squatted down beside me with his little case and the injection he had prepared.

But I now felt entirely at the mercy of fate and had decided on a different course.

In a calm voice that surprised even me, I told him my thoughts.

"Look, it is very kind of you to be willing to give me this injection. But I can see that this time they *are* sending people off when they're not fit for transport—even fever cases. You know what I think? If I am destined to go off into the unknown with this transport, I'd prefer to go well and strong, rather than ill. I will have a better chance at the end of the journey, or wherever we go after that, if I'm healthy. So thanks for everything. You did what you could."

Pepík was speechless, partly in sudden despair over what was going to happen to me, but partly because he felt I was probably right. He sat by me for a moment longer. "Whatever you think. I won't force you. When it comes to a decisive moment, everyone knows best where his own strength lies."

"Fantlová Zdenka!" We both heard it this time. No fresh cases were being brought in. Suddenly I had a brainstorm. It was as if some unknown power had surged up inside me and was telling me what to do—a last-minute instinct of self-preservation.

"Pepík," I burst out. "I have an idea. Marta—she's the only one who can help me now. Go to the Dresden barracks quickly and find her. She isn't on duty tonight. Ask her to come here right away and bring a nurse's uniform with her, wrapped up. Please, Pepík, hurry! We have very little time."

He agreed and ran out through the door.

The clock now showed 3:45 A.M. *They'll take me, they'll take me not. They'll take me, they'll take me not,* the clock seemed to chant softly.

"Fantlová Zdenka," echoed hollowly through the nearly empty hall. My life was at the cliff edge now, and my heart was beating so loudly I was afraid the officials would hear it. Time was running out. If Marta failed to come, I was doomed.

At that moment she appeared in the doorway, deus ex machina. Wearing her nurse's uniform, she came straight to me. There was no time for friendly exchanges.

"Help me to the toilet," I said. "It's at the end of the corridor."

Supporting me like a sick patient, she slowly led me along. We both walked into the stall and bolted the door. With lightning speed I put the spare uniform on over my nightdress. We decided to walk straight out of the barracks together, like two nurses on duty. Fortune favors the brave and the daring.

We ran downstairs to the corridor where there were still a few SS men standing around. Arm in arm, we exchanged lively talk and even laughed a little to show how casually we were going off duty. I shivered inwardly, but we passed them calmly enough and went out through the barracks gate into the street. We had won. The miracle had happened. I was free for the moment. But what next? We had to stop after the next corner and try to calm ourselves down.

It was not over yet, however. The total count of the transport had to tally exactly with the names and numbers on the list and everything was rigorously checked. The death penalty for attempted escape from a transport applied equally to failure to report. My name had not yet been taken off the list. Marta came to a decision. One of the doctors on duty there was a close friend of her husband, Karel.

"Wait here for me," she said. "I will go back there and explain that I have to speak to him urgently."

As a nurse she could enter the barracks freely. She found a chance to have a quick word with the doctor, who promised her he would get my name taken off, which he managed to do at his own risk.

I vanished from the list and from that transport.

At 5 A.M., with all the coaches locked, the train pulled away. It was not until after the war that I found out where it had gone. It had gone to Auschwitz, and all of its passengers, without exception, were taken straight to the gas chambers.

18. THE WOODS AT KŘIVOKLÁT

Christmas and New Year's slipped across the calendar and sank like the weak winter sun below the horizon. We had been in Terezín for a year. Apart from Father, we were all still together: Grandmother, Mother, Brother, Sister, and me. Gradually we were forgetting our old home. Life was so different here. There were lots of us, all supporting one another in the hope and longing that we would survive and hold out in this place until the end of the war. We all tried to live normally, however abnormal the conditions.

There was no shortage of fresh developments, and new regulations were announced every day. But no one ever expected good tidings. However, one day an announcement ran through the ghetto which for a while lit up the surrounding gloom like a brief flash of sun breaking merrily through a gray pall of clouds.

> ONE THOUSAND YOUNG WOMEN ARE TO VOLUN-
> TEER TOMORROW FOR TREE PLANTING IN THE
> KŘIVOKLÁT WOODS. FOR ONE MONTH. DEPARTURE
> IN TWO DAYS TIME.

I jumped for joy and decided to enroll immediately. An excursion from Terezín to the Bohemian forest sounded like a month's holiday. My decision, and my evident delight, nearly made Mother collapse.

"You must be crazy! At a time and place like this no one rushes into anything voluntarily. How do you know where they'll take you? They may promise you all sorts of things, but you can't trust the Germans. You stay put. I forbid you to go."

But the passage of time had changed the rules of our game. We weren't at home anymore, where Mother could exercise her authority. That had gone by the boards. I was almost twenty-one and making decisions for myself. Still, I tried to reassure her.

"Don't worry, they obviously need us very badly for this tree planting. You'll see. Everything will turn out all right, and I will be back in a month."

I couldn't wait to see the green trees and smell their aroma. I signed up and in two days was off with the others by train to Křivoklát—exactly as they promised.

They split us up into groups of fifty girls each. My group was housed in a large log cabin deep in the forest. In front of it was a little hut for two gendarmes who were there to guard us. They were middle-aged men, quite friendly and jolly it seemed to me. They even smiled at us. We all spoke Czech and felt as if we were on a school field trip.

The forestry authorities attached an experienced man to our group who explained the situation. "The job we've got, girls, is to replant some large areas of forest that have been clear-cut. You'll be given a fresh supply of seedlings every day. I'll be coming for you at seven o'clock to take you to the site. There I'll show you how to plant young conifers. I hope you like it here. And now goodbye until I come for you tomorrow."

The following day we set out for the planting site at a brisk pace. It was all quite unreal. Terezín was forgotten. All the fortifications and uniformed SS men disappeared from our minds— even the war raging across Europe. Only the beautiful green trees remained, silent and peaceful, ethereal. They carried a whiff of eternity, quite detached from all that was going on around them. The smell of sap, pine needles, and moss was intoxicating.

We worked hard all day and sank into healthy sleep each night in our bunks. How we loved it there. We regretted that we couldn't spend the rest of our days in this quiet paradise until the war was over. One day, after we came back from work, one of the gendarmes came into our cabin, which he normally never did, and asked in a severe official tone, "Is there a Fantlová Zdenka among you?"

I swallowed hard. Why would anybody be looking for me here? Could it have anything to do with my escape from the transport group? It all seemed rather alarming. I hesitated for a moment. My neighbor, who knew my name, looked at me questioningly. I realized there was no escape.

The gendarme stared hard at us all and waited.

"Well," he repeated, "is the girl in question here or isn't she?"

"Yes," I sighed and half raised my hand.

"Come with me, then," said the gendarme.

I staggered out as if never to return. When we arrived at the police hut he motioned me to go in. He followed me and shut the door behind us.

"Look," he said, "some middle aged civilian turned up around midday and told us he'd heard a rumor going around that there were some girls from Terezín working here. And if there was a certain Fantlová Zdenka among them, as I now know there is, would we allow him to leave something here for her. He didn't give a name; he said it didn't matter. So here it is. Take it back with you to Terezín when you return there in a couple of days." Crossing over to the corner of the room he handed me a heavy case. "We have no objection to your having it," he said.

This was a quite unexpected turn of events. My fears evaporated and I now felt so deeply touched by the humanity and self sacrifice of the thing that I could find no words. It could only have been one man, Matysek, my father's old assistant, who had always been so fond of us, as we of him. He used to take me to school and called me Sumbalka.

I took the case back to our log cabin and opened it. It was full of treasures: clothes, underwear, stockings, soap, bread, two tins of dripping, biscuits, and lump sugar—anything he could manage to lay his hands on. It must have been an enormous expense, effort, and sacrifice. Here in Křivoklát we weren't starving, but I gave each of the girls something.

When we left two days later, the gendarmes and the forester came to say goodbye and wish us a safe journey. I arrived back in Terezín with my case, looking as if I had just come from abroad. No one asked me any questions. My mother, brother, and sister were all delighted—to have me back and to see my case with everything inside it.

Matysek's generosity raised my spirits. How heart warming it was to know that there were good people still around even in the worst of times.

19. "CAN YOU CRY, MISS?"

Back in Terezín I immediately resumed my place in the kitchen and was soon re-accustomed to the old routine and discipline. During my absence, several of our group had been sent east. New people had taken their places among the kitchen staff, dishing out food and punching meal slips.

Among them was a pale young man in a belted raincoat and blue beret. He had big eyes and looked like the sad Pierrot from traditional Italian pantomime. I had no idea then of his name or what he had been doing before he came to Terezín. One day there were hundreds of people in the soup line impatiently waiting to be served. I was on duty, standing with my ladle at the ready and waiting for the *parták* to give the word. This pale young man stood beside me with his tool for punching the meal tickets.

Suddenly he turned to me and said, "Excuse me, miss. Can you cry?"

I wondered why I should be asked such an unusual question but answered without much hesitation. "Mmm, yes, I can."

"Right, then. Come along to the Magdeburg barracks this evening to our play rehearsal. We're trying something new, our own cabaret, *Prince Confined-to-Bed,* something I wrote with a friend. My name's Josef Lustig."

I soon found out that Josef Lustig was an established actor and playwright, best known, despite his appearance, for comedy and satirical cabaret.

Such was my entrée to the world of the stage—in Terezín.

The theater in Terezín had a modest, gingerly start, slinking in on tiptoe, as it were. Among the inmates were many well-known Czech actors, directors, stage designers, writers, and artists, as well as professional musicians, conductors, and composers. There was no shortage of artistic talent.

Many people had a deep yearning to express themselves artistically, both in words and music, and the rest welcomed the results with gratitude as a compensation for their confinement. Every cultural event buoyed up their hopes and morale and reinforced their faith in human values. High culture spilled over from prewar civilized life, but in these trying and uncertain conditions it acquired a deeper significance.

It started with solo performances on the top floors of the barracks—sometimes poetry recitals, sometimes readings from works of literature people had brought along in their suitcases. Soon came dramatic fragments involving several voices. The first efforts were cautious and halting, as though the actors were testing the ice to see if it would bear their weight. The thought in everyone's mind was simply, What will the Germans think?

Surprisingly, the Germans had no objection at all to these innocent experiments. On the contrary, they gave their official blessing to what they named *Kamaradenabende,* "friendly evenings." From that point on, artistic activity in Terezín grew by leaps and bounds. Little stages were constructed in the attics with wings and curtains; then benches were set out in front of them—instant theater. Some of the plays were imported from the outside, some written by the inmates themselves. Theatrical companies were formed, with separate groups specializing in different genres. Directors were on tap, backdrops were painted, and costumes made from whatever was available—burlap, bedsheets, paper, scraps of old clothing.

The same sort of thing happened with music. Instruments, sheet music, and scores appeared from nowhere. Enough talent was discovered to assemble a jazz band, then a string quartet, a choir, and even a symphony orchestra.

Everyone gave their best, whatever their ability.

There were no names in neon lights, no fame, no fortune—only the satisfaction of a job well done and the appreciation of a grateful audience. To this end professionals and amateurs worked hand in hand, free of envy and self-importance.

I turned up punctually that evening at Magdeburg barracks, feeling rather important and special now that I was moving in artistic circles.

Josef Lustig was standing on the stage, talking to his friend and collaborator, Jirí Sřpitz. Karel Kowanitz was with them too. He had written the lyrics for the songs that comprised the show. They had decided to base their cabaret on the style of the famous Voskovec and Werich partners, so that the Terezín Theater would be a miniature version of the radical Liberated Theater in Prague. The content would be allegorical. Between the scenes Lustig and Sřpitz, dressed as clowns, would deliver topical commentary in front of the curtain, punctuated with songs set to the original theater music but with new lyrics of their own.

Their play *Prince Confined-to-Bed* was a fairy tale allegory set in the reign of King Gumboil XII, featuring his son, Prince Confined-to-Bed, and his daughter, Princess Off-Duty. The palace scenes were done like a puppet play with jerky movements and squeaky voices, a takeoff of the "puppet government" that ran the Terezín camp. The audience cheered wildly at every satirical scene or remark.

The action of the play was quite simple. Prince Confined-to-Bed falls ill and is declared by his doctor unfit for work and hence for transport. But the wicked magician releases him from bed so he can join the transport. At that point a young girl in the audience bursts into tears over the Prince's plight. Hearing this, the clowns invite her onstage and assure her that the Prince is going to stay bedridden and everything will turn out all right.

I was supposed to take the part of the tearful girl. I promised to give it my best.

Rehearsals proceeded. On cue I was supposed to, at first, sob quietly and then to weep out loud. On the opening night they put me among the audience in the third row. No one took any notice of me, and the play began. Every seat in the attic auditorium was filled.

But things went all wrong. When my cue came and I began quietly sobbing, everyone around me tried to shut me up. "Sh-h-h!" "Don't interrupt!" "For chrissake be quiet!"

I went on howling, waiting desperately for the clowns to rescue me with their line, "Hang on! What's that young lady crying about?" and fetching me out of the audience. Whereupon the audience would sigh with relief and realize it was all part of the play.

However, nothing of the kind happened. The clowns had decided to build up the tension. Meanwhile, the fire marshal in the doorway took action. With one leap he rushed up and started dragging me outside as a disrupter. Not wanting to spoil the play, I went on crying while hissing at him between my teeth, "I'm part of the play!"

That didn't impress him at all. "Oh yeah? Just come along quietly!"

At that moment a voice came from the stage. "Hang on! What's that young lady crying about?"

The fire marshal was oblivious. His job was to keep law and order, and I was already halfway out the door. There was now great commotion among the spectators, who were not sure what was going on. At the very last moment one of the clowns jumped down and hauled me back, to the audience's great relief. And mine.

It wasn't an easy role. At the second performance things went quite differently. On the given cue I started sobbing, and then crying out loud. Across the gangway an elderly man was sitting with a case on his lap, evidently a doctor. He jumped up, took out his instruments, and was on the point of giving me a sedative for hysteria. Just in time, the actors onstage saw what was happening and came to my rescue.

Each evening there was some new incident. But the word got around quickly, and after a few days everyone in Terezín knew about this girl who cried in the audience. In the end, people started looking around long before my scene was due and laughing prematurely. "Watch, now. That girl in the third row's going to start crying any moment, ho-ho-ho."

If it hadn't been for the fact that transports to the East took place at irregular intervals so that uncertainty hung over our heads like the sword of Damocles, we could almost have fancied we were living normal lives. The Germans began actively to support our cultural efforts and, at the same time, to exploit them for propaganda purposes. Hitler had "given the Jews an independent city," they claimed. True, we had more freedom of movement inside the fortified walls of Terezín than outside. But it was all a hoax.

They had their own plans for our future, which they kept strictly to themselves. They had condemned us to death, but they allowed us to play and sing until the end. Why shouldn't they? The smiles would soon be wiped from our faces. So we all carried on, dancing under the gallows.

Thus from the unlikely but supremely fertile soil of overcrowded Terezín, amidst wretched hunger, fear, and constant death—but also amid hope and a refusal to succumb to pain and humiliation—there arose an unprecedented theatrical and musical culture of the highest quality.

The Czech theater in the ghetto was no mere entertainment, or social distraction, but a living torch that showed people the way ahead and lent them spiritual strength and hope. For many, cultural experience became more important than a ration of bread.

I felt at home among those actors and artists. In addition to their eight-hour workday, they threw themselves into acting, rehearsing, and writing. Their ranks included many men and women of exceptional talent and ability. No sooner had they arrived in Terezín, that they fit into its cultural life, stamping its plays and concerts with their individual genius, and raising its creative standards to extraordinary heights.

One such man was Karel Švenk, writer, composer, choreographer, actor, and clown—something of a Czech Chaplin. He was about twenty-five, and his twinkling eyes under bushy black brows radiated energy. He wrote, acted, and emceed his own cabaret. Unlike Lustig and Sřpitz with their domestic topics, Švenk's satires were markedly political. In his first revue, *Long Live Life*, complete with mime and ballet, Švenk played the part of a persecuted clown.

What achieved overnight fame, however, was the closing song, which had a jolly marching rhythm. It gave voice to the suppressed longings of every inmate, and we promptly adopted it as our Terezín anthem:

> *Where there's a will there's always a way*
> *So hand in hand we start,*
> *Whatever the trials of the day*
> *There's laughter in our heart.*
> *Day after day we go on our way*
> *From one place to another,*
> *We're only allowed thirty words to a letter*
> *But hey, tomorrow life starts again*
> *And that's a day nearer to when we can pack*

And leave for home with a bag on our back.
Where there's a will there's always a way
So hold hands now, hold them fast,
And over the ghetto's ruins we
Shall laugh aloud at last.

And this is how we all honestly believed things would end up.

Švenk's second production, *The Last Cyclist*, had a definite plot and a provocatively anti-Nazi message. The story was roughly this: All the madmen and psychopaths in some imaginary country rebel and escape from their asylums. After causing a public uproar, they seize the reins of government. They are led by a ruler called The Rat. To find a scapegoat for all the misrule and shortages they have caused, they pick on one group of people who can be blamed for everything—cyclists.

Cyclists, they say, are the root of all evil and responsible for everything that has gone wrong. Cyclists are, moreover, a dangerous element backed by an international conspiracy. The country must get rid of them. A list of all cyclists has to be compiled, except for those who can prove that their ancestors over the last six generations were all pedestrians. All cyclists are to be caught and loaded on board a ship and taken to the Island of Horror.

Among the deportees is one Borivoj Abeles. Leaning over the railings he loses his balance and falls into the water. He starts swimming toward the nearest shore and thinks he is now safe. The madmen see him, however, fish him out, and lock him in a cage in the zoo, where he is exhibited as the Last Cyclist. But the Rat has other ideas. He orders the country to rid itself of this last cyclist. He is to be put into a rocket and shot into outer space. When everything is ready for takeoff, the Rat and his female companion, the Lady, go on board with her staff to inspect the rocket. They grant Borivoj Abeles one last wish. He asks to be allowed a cigarette.

He strikes a match and absentmindedly, instead of lighting his cigarette, puts the match to the fuse of the rocket. The rocket hurtles off, along with the Rat, the Lady, and her staff, while Borivoj stands watching it disappear into the wide blue yonder.

The Last Cyclist somehow eluded German censorship, but its effect on the audience was like dynamite. However, its run was cut short. When the members of the Council of Elders came to see it, they were horror-struck by its obviously provocative allegory and banned it.

Many of the inmates had already had a chance to enjoy the play, but many others were denied the pleasure. Its story became part of Terezín legend, and the courageous Karel Švenk became a local hero.

20. WAS BEN AKIBA A LIAR?

Over the course of 1943 it seemed that transports to the East had become considerably fewer. Then they came to a halt. Part of the explanation was that the German government had transferred one sector of its war production to Terezín and needed all available manpower. The sector in question involved delaminating mica for military purposes. Wooden cabins were quickly erected for hundreds of workers, mostly women, who sat all day splitting sheets of mica.

The constant fear of being transported to the East suddenly abated, and a period of calm spread through the ghetto. A rumor began to circulate that, according to reports from abroad, the German front was retreating and the war would be over in two months. How eager we all were to believe this! But two months went by and the war still wasn't over. Hopes were then transferred to the next two months, and the next. So time went on. Somehow one could always survive two months at a time.

The time seemed appropriate for further theatrical experiments. Lustig and Sřpitz assembled a sizable body of actors for a new play, *Ben Akiba Was No Liar—Or Was He?*

The play, or rather cabaret, features two clowns disputing the wisdom of the legendary Rabbi Ben Akiba in his famous pronouncement that "There is nothing new under the sun. Everything has happened before."

The first clown sets out to convince his partner that every event is merely a repetition of some earlier one, albeit in different form and circumstance, so there is really nothing new under the sun. To prove the point he transports him through time to a Roman circus where Christian prisoners are being thrown to the lions. One of the victims is Mordecai Pinchas. He tries to explain to the hungry lion that it is all a mistake, since he is a Jew and not a Christian at all. The lion sniffs him and finds no difference. Mordecai starts to negotiate and addresses the lion.

"Mr. Leo, sir, Mr. Levi, sir, be reasonable, I shouldn't be here at all, I'm Jewish." After a long argument he persuades the lion there has been an organizational mix-up and is allowed to leave the arena.

"You see?" the second clown bursts in. "Now *that* has *never* happened before." So Ben Akiba *was* lying.

Between this scene and the next the clowns come to the front of the stage and start delving into Czech history with a punning dialogue in the manner of Voskovec and Werich interludes. "Taking things from the very beginning, then, we have the ancestor of all Czechs, the Grand Ancestor, Cech, standing on Řípa Hill, stretching his arm out to the sun and declaring: This is the land overflowing with milk and mead, *tato zeme oplévá mlékem a strdím.*"

"Sorry to interrupt you . . . really sorry . . . but could you please tell me exactly what this 'mead' is?"

"I *beg* your pardon? You've never heard of mead?"

"Terribly sorry . . . but honestly . . . I never really *have* known what 'mead' is."

"Ought to be ashamed. Everyone knows what mead is, any child can tell you."

"Any child, yes . . . yes . . . but me, I've no idea."

"Have you never seen it written up in front of a restaurant? Like today's special, sour mead?"

"Not really, no."

"For goodness sake, man, how can I explain? Mead is simply . . . well . . . mead, isn't it? So let's not waste anymore time and get on with the next stage in Czech history. The ancient Czechs were a very advanced people who burnt their dead and put their ashes *do uren umne zdobenych,* into artistically decorated urns."

Second clown (pretending he heard the phonetically identical *do uren u mne zdobenych,* "urns decorated in my house"): "Is that so, now? I never realized you did your business in urns as well as textiles!"

"No, you've got me wrong. I said *umne,* artistically like."

"Oh, well, if it was done in your place I've no doubt it was very artistic."

The word play continues circularly, which the audiences loved.

The "mead" episode was particularly successful and people were forever buttonholing each other when they met and repeating parts of the dialogue. Two venerable members of the Council of Elders were even overheard conversing in the corridor:

"Very amusing, that bit about 'mead' in the Ben Akiba piece, wasn't it?"

"Indeed."

"But tell me, professor, what actually is mead?"

"You don't mean to say you don't know?"

And so it went on, all around the town. No one knew what mead was.

Scene Two is set on Olympus, where the gods are holding council around a table, arguing and failing to agree about anything. Zeus is in the chair, trying to moderate. Their quarrels were meant to echo the divisions within both the Council of Elders and the German political leadership. I played the part of Aphrodite. Instead of just being pretty and quietly seducing all the gods, she keeps on interfering, correcting the others, and disrupting the proceedings.

Scene Three is set in Heaven, where the Empress Maria Theresa and her son Joseph are sitting on a cloud, looking down through a telescope. What should come swimming into their field of view but Terezín, the town they founded as a fortress against the Prussians. They look harder and harder, but the place seems so unfamiliar. What could have happened to it? they speculate.

Then suddenly two Jewish souls come floating up straight from Terezín and offer to give the empress and her son a detailed account of events down there. But their majesties reject it out of hand. From which the Second Clown deduces that what is now happening in the fortress is truly unprecedented. So Ben Akiba *was* lying.

One of the theme songs running through the cabaret was written by František Kowanitz to the tune of Jaroslav Jezek's famous satirical song "Civilization."

> *A certain ruler issued a decree,*
> *As we can read in any History,*
> *Fearing attack by enemies afar*
> *To build a fortress city like a star.*
> *To make invasion really difficult*
> *He had a ring of mighty earthworks built*
> *With creeks and coves to each redoubt*
> *And moats and ditches roundabout*
> *Plus soldiery within the walls*
> *To fire their cannon balls.*
> *The citizens were super posh,*
> *Prime pork and haggis was their nosh,*
> *They loved to sing pub songs, and those*
> *Were meant to terrify their foes.*
>
> *But many years have passed since then,*
> *The world has somewhat changed its face,*
> *And since the town inspired no dread*
> *Word came that those of a certain race*

Must all wear stars and live inside
By thousands, filling every shop, wall, inn,
Barracks and café, till there was no space,
No food, and anyone was glad
To eat the odd potatoskin.
Rations were short because there was a crisis,
No booze, no cash for paying silly prices,
When suddenly the town's true role
In a new light was seen
To serve as propaganda both
In newspapers and on the screen.

In view of the last-mentioned revelation
There now arose a new organization,
New insights and new points of view,
New parties and new leaders too.
All labor was deployed by Hundertschaften,
A Raumwirtschaft saw to each inmate's comfort,
Verteilungsstellen issued them fine clothes,
Bettenbau got them snug asleep at night,
Entwesung saw to bodily hygiene, and
Freizeitgestaltung put their souls aright.

All the organizations with German names mentioned in the last verse really existed and saw to it that life went on in Terezín in as orderly a way as possible.

The *Hundertschaft* was a labor unit of one hundred men.

The *Raumwirtschaft* allocated living space in the billets.

The *Verteilungsstelle* collected clothes from those who died, sorted them, and "sold" them in shops set up for the purpose.

Bettenbau was a carpentry shop that made bunks, partitions, and "furniture" for the elite in their penthouses and cubby holes.

Entwesung was the delousing and disinfecting station. The Germans were obsessed by the danger of epidemics of any kind.

Freizeitgestaltung, "leisure structuring," was a new department within the self-governing administration that had arisen during the great cultural upsurge and dealt with all its requirements. It authorized new sites (mainly in the attics) for plays and concerts, organized scientific and literary talks, assigned rehearsal time to pianists on the two available pianos, allocated materials for scenery, and printed theater and concert programs and tickets. It was responsible for the choice of dramatic material for performance.

Freizeitgestaltung was also concerned with leisure time sports, of which the most popular was soccer. This was played even in the most cramped barracks courtyards. Every male barracks had its own team, so one would find, for example Sudeten trying to get the better of Hannover. Matches were fought with as much verve as if international cups were at stake, and around the hastily prepared playing fields the galleries were packed with fans on every floor.

Music occupied an even larger place than the theater in our cultural life. Terezín was awash with outstanding musical performers, conductors, and composers. The famous Prague conductor Karel Ančerl, who used to stir soup beside me in the kitchen during his working hours, organized a string quartet in his free time and, later on, a complete orchestra.

The composer Hans Krása, already established before the war, made his name in Terezín with his unique children's opera, *Brundibár.* This was a musical fairy tale played and sung by children in the camp between eight and twelve years old. It was rehearsed and performed countless times both for children and adult audiences in the Sokol Hall. The story was simple and topical:

Two little children, Pepícek (Joey) and Anna, find that their mother is ill. They would like to get her some milk, but they have no money. So they decide to sing in the streets in the hope of earning enough to buy some. They sing their best and passersby throw coins into their cap. But then along comes the wicked organ grinder Brundibár, who tries to stop them and steals their cap with all the money. With the help of some animals—a dog, a cat, and a sparrow—they overcome Brundibár and chase him off. Justice has been done and the piece ends with the children's chorus

> *Nad Brundibárem jsme vyhrály, my jsme se nebály.*
> We fought old Brundibár and won, because we
> weren't afraid.

The young performers and their audiences were equally thrilled. I remember squeezing into the hall where the seats and all standing room were crammed full. Lovely, healthy, talented kids they were, and all of them prisoners. Their eyes shone with excitement at the fall of wicked Brundibár.

That was in September 1943.

Soon afterward came the order to resume the transports. Most of the children who had so merrily performed in *Brundibár* were sent to their fate in the East. End of fairy tale.

Several of our *Ben Akiba* cast were sent off as well, and we had to suspend the cabaret. In the end we were never able to perform it again because our treasured Josef Lustig's tuberculosis suddenly got worse. He lay in the sick bay in Kavalírka barracks. I used to visit him as often as I could and, as a little treat, I took him part of my own ration from the kitchen. There were no medicines. He knew he would never live to see his home again.

When I was sitting on his bed one day, Josef said to me, "You remember the first time I ever spoke to you, and asked you, 'Can you cry, miss?' Well, when I die, don't cry. If you survive, you must tell people how we kept the show going in Terezín."

Two days later he died. When I went to see him they were just carrying him out of the room, wrapped in a sheet.

Our group then dissolved, having completed its mission: to use satire to project the truth, while trying to give the audiences some moral support and hope.

Not long after Josef's death, his inseparable colleague, fellow writer, and fellow actor Jirí Sřpitz was also taken off somewhere to the East. I sat with him until the early hours before he was loaded into the cattle car, helping him sort out the few things he was taking with him. We speculated about where he might be going. We had just enough time to sing Švenk's Terezín anthem to ourselves:

> *Where there's a will there's always a way.*
> *So hold hands now, hold them fast,*
> *And over the ghetto's ruins we*
> *Shall laugh aloud at last.*

And then he was off.

In the darkness of Terezín our cabaret had been like a sparkler on a Christmas tree that lights up and dazzles for a brief moment and then suddenly goes out. But everyone who saw it retained in his mind's eye the memory of its short, vivid brilliance.

21. THE POTEMKIN VILLAGE FACADE

Miraculously, my own family, except for Father, had managed to hold together. Jírka had been on shift work in the bakery for some time, and whenever he got a special ration he would bring some back as a treat for Mother.

Mother was still in the Hamburg billet where we were assigned when we arrived, but alone now with Lydia—Lidá, as I had begun to call her. I was in my cubby hole, my little train compartment, and came back to see Mother whenever I had a free moment. She was sad and anxious.

One day our grandmother was put on the transport list. There was no appeal. Sick as she was, she had to go east. God knows why the Germans could not have let the elderly, at least, stay on in Terezín instead of shifting them in these insufferable transport trains to unknown destinations where they would die anyway. It was a bitter, cruel leave-taking.

Soon another transport included the room leader of Mother's billet, so that a successor had to be elected. They chose Mother. This was her salvation. She now had plenty to worry about, maintaining order, keeping the billet quiet and tidy, dividing up the bread ration, and so forth.

My sister Lidá worked with other youngsters on the ramparts, growing tomatoes for the German garrison. But they weren't allowed to touch them and they were very strictly checked. As she was working apart from me, we didn't see much of each other. Sometimes she sneaked into the audience to see a play I was in. I was always glad to see her, although I noticed she seemed more interested in Petr, the boy who was operating the lights, than she was in my performance.

Then one day news spread that a thousand male volunteers were being taken for work outside Terezín, in the Kladno coal mines. My brother signed up. Mother protested, just as she had when I went tree planting in Křivoklát. But he went all the same, with a large group of young men, and at the appointed time they all returned.

Mother sighed with relief to see him back. He himself would much rather have stayed in Kladno, but he had no choice.

Time moved on. We had grown accustomed to the Terezín routine and forgotten our old home. In fact, we no longer felt we were even entitled to remember it. Other things were more important, like not getting listed for transport and staying alive until the war ended. Surely sometime it must end.

Daily life in Terezín was a continuous kaleidoscope. New transports arrived and were sorted out into work groups, old people died, the artistic crowd put on plays and concerts, transports left for the East, lovers hid where they could, more people died, orphans survived on their own in children's blocks. . . . We waited and waited, trying to hold on until the end.

I missed Arno badly. He had been gone for nearly two years. Where might he be? Was he alone or with his brother? What was he doing? Was he in a camp? Working outside, or in a factory? How was he being treated? Was he in good health and determined to hang on to the end? After all, we were going to find each other as soon as the war was over and start a happy new life amid peace and affection—and forget there had ever been a war.

But no answers came. Here and there words were dropped—"Auschwitz"; "Birkenau"—but no one knew anything definite. It was all guesswork.

Among the Terezín inmates was an old clairvoyant who claimed to know what had happened to those who went east.

When she sought inspiration she had to hold something in her hand that had belonged to the lost one. I went to consult her with the ring Arno had made for me, the one tangible thing that linked us together. I trembled to hear what she might say. She sat in her chair with her eyes shut, turning the ring in her hand. My heart thumped as I waited for her answer.

"I can't find him anywhere," she said softly. "All I can see is the letter *T*. Nothing else."

I went off, rather relieved that she had told me nothing definite or devastating. I remained convinced that, wherever he was, Arno would find in himself the strength to survive.

In the spring of 1944, the German leadership invited an international commission to visit Terezín to see for themselves the "paradise" that the Führer had designed for the Jews. The local command accordingly ordered a campaign of embellishment. Feverish preparations were initiated. The streets and squares that the commission would be passing through had to be thoroughly spruced up.

So that the ghetto should not appear overcrowded, 7,000 wretched inhabitants were immediately sent to the East.

A café was constructed on the main square where selected inmates could be seen drinking coffee and eating cakes while a jazz orchestra, the Ghetto Swingers, played for their pleasure. Grass was ordered to be sown and flowering shrubs planted around the edge of the square, where benches would be set up for people to sit and make lively conversation. An orchestra would play in a new gazebo in the center of town.

Paths were cleaned up for selected prisoners to take leisurely strolls. New playgrounds with swings and other delights were laid out for the children.

The facades of houses in designated streets were given a fresh coat of whitewash and their windows fitted with curtains. Shop windows were quickly cleared of those who had been billeted in them and were soon tastefully decorated with goods removed from the luggage of new arrivals.

Once I passed such a window being rearranged by the well-known stage artist and designer František "Honza" Zelenka.

"Hello, Honza," I said. "What are you doing here?"

He took a few steps back and eyed his work critically. "Just adding a few meaningless touches," he answered, with a dismissive wave of the hand.

A model troupe of pretty girls, including Lidá, were ordered to cross the square carrying rakes over their shoulders and strolling to a tune, as if finishing a day's gardening.

Inmates from the children's homes were to be seen crowding around Lagerkommandant Rahm, the German officer in charge of Terezín. He would hand out tins of sardines while they recited well learned lines: "Oh, not sardines again, Uncle Rahm!"

The day before the commission was due, a squad of women was assembled with brooms, cloths, and pails of water, who then knelt and scrubbed the pavements until they shone like mirrors. We weren't allowed to walk on them that day.

The eminent visitors arrived as planned and drove in open cars through the specially beautified streets and squares. Everything went perfectly. Haggard figures sat on the new benches, melancholy faces stared from the cafés. Karel Ančerl conducted his orchestra in the concert hall, and in the Sokol Hall a choir directed by Raphael Schächter sang Verdi's *Requiem*. The international commission left, thoroughly convinced of the authenticity of the Terezín paradise. Immediately after the inspection several new transports were assembled to leave for the East, including most of the children who, only a few days before, had been so realistically thanking Kommandant Rahm for their sardines.

22. THE CZECH THEATER CARRIES ON

The theatrical world of Terezín could never have functioned without the activity behind the scenes by the enormously experienced and ingenious František Zelenka. Architect and stage designer by training, he had made his name long before the war with his avant-garde sets for leading Prague stages, including the Liberated Theater.

When he had come to Terezín in 1943, he threw himself into theater work, which was enjoying its golden age at that time. He had his own workshop where backdrops were set up and painted, stage properties constructed, and costumes designed and created. He had to make bricks without straw. He used any material that came his way—paper, sawdust, rags, empty tins, old sheets—and achieved miracles with it. His skill was responsible for the brilliant design of the children's opera *Brundibár* and of the stage productions that followed.

He worked closely with that most able of directors, Gustav Schorsch, who had been an assistant director of the National Theater in Prague before coming to Terezín. Schorsch was a theatrical purist, a pedagogue and theoretician of the old school, and would tolerate no departure from the highest standards. Using a group of young Prague professional players and Zelenka's designs, he put on a production of Gogol's *Wedding* that would have won acclaim anywhere in the world.

In his "spare time" Gustav organized recitals of Czech poetry and held a seminar for young actors. After the great success of *Wedding* he started working on a play by Griboyedov but had to abandon it after a few rehearsals, when some of his cast were sent East. The same fate attended his planned production of Shakespeare's

Twelfth Night, after his remaining actors were swallowed up in a new wave of transports.

After the dispersal of Lustig's cabaret group, the few of us who remained had been transferred to other projects. One of these was Štech's *Tretí Zvonení*, Third Time Lucky, and soon after that the actress Vlasta Schönová started rehearsals for František Langer's comedy *Velbloud Uchem Jehly*, A Camel Through the Eye of a Needle. It was the mere coincidence of both texts turning up in Terezín that made it possible to produce these two lighthearted plays, familiar from prewar days. They were given a great welcome and for one evening, at least, revived memories of happier times in better places.

The director-writer Norbert Frýd and the composer Karel Reiner had arrived in Terezín sometime in 1943. Each worked in his own field with E. F. Burian and his avant-garde *Divadlo D*, Theater D, in Prague. Norbert Frýd brought with him in his luggage the text of a biblical folk play, *Esther*, which had been rehearsed under Burian but never reached the stage. The Terezín theater world seemed to have been waiting for these two men, who both got down to work immediately. Frýd took on the production and Reiner composed original music for it. He would sit at his little piano in front of the stage extemporizing half-tone melodies as the play proceeded.

Franta Zelenka in turn took on the staging and costume designs. They made a happy trio. *Esther* was a contrast to all the other plays staged in Terezín. For a start, it was written in verse, and in near-medieval Czech at that.

The production completely dispensed with realism and was imaginatively stylized. The story itself, telling how Queen Esther saved her Jewish tribe from certain annihilation, was deeply meaningful for Terezín and its inhabitants.

Rehearsals went ahead at a feverish pace, and the production began to take shape. Out of nothing, Zelenka produced sets that would have done credit to any theater of international standing. The whole backdrop was a semicircle of "straw" to lend pastoral color. There were three separate tents on the stage with sackcloth curtains. Sitting in each one was a leading character: the king in the middle tent, the queen on the right, and Mordecai on the left. The Narrator, stick in hand, walks around in front of the tents and tells the story.

Then with his stick he pulls aside the curtain of one tent, announcing: "And the King said or the Queen, or Mordecai," as the plot develops.

Zelenka dreamed up quite ravishing costumes. King Ahazverus was put into a white sheet, cut out in the middle for his head, and empty tins were sewn onto the bottom hem so that they tinkled when he walked.

"When you cross the stage," Zelenka explained, "I want to hear the cans rattling against each other."

On his head the king wore a cut out paper crown, with blobs of auburn colored sawdust stuck on to his head and forearms. He carried a whip stock in his hand and looked very impressive.

Zelenka dressed Haman's wife Zeresh in loose-flowing multi-colored robes. "I want you," he said, "to look like some figure flying through a window display in Ascher's House of Silk on Mustek in the middle of Prague." Which is just what she did look like.

I played the part of Queen Vashti. Zelenka dressed me in two sheets sewn together, the inside one white, the outer dyed black. The outer one had large peacock eyes cut out of it, so that the white undersheet showed through. His instructions were simple: "When you walk along the stage and the clothes flap around you, I want you to look like a baroque angel over a grave."

And thus it appeared. He was full of ingenious ideas and humorous fancies.

The *Esther* production, however well rehearsed and well received, finally fell victim to another series of transports. When several of the cast were taken off, the end was inevitable. With a heavy heart, Nóra told us he could not embark on fresh rehearsals with new actors. So that was the end of *Esther* in the little Magdeburg theater.

But it was certainly a vintage production and retains a lasting place in the memories of the participants and of those spectators who had the chance to see it.

After the collapse of *Esther,* another director, Otakar Ruzicka, decided to put on the Molière comedy *Georges Dandin.* This only needed a small cast, and I was assigned the part of the society lady Madame de Sottenville, starchly buttonedup with monocle permanently poised.

The rehearsals went badly and Ruzicka gave up. He was succeeded by Zelenka who was willing to take on directing as well as stage management. Production was transferred to the larger and better equipped stage in the Dresden barracks top floor, where there was room for a larger audience too. But despite these advantages the play was a flop. Whether it was the fault of the production or the weakness of the play itself, Molière and his subject didn't fit into the Terezín of those years.

So even though none of the cast was lost to the transports this time, the play closed.

I now found myself with evenings free and was finally able to enjoy one of the many concerts that Terezín now offered. I chose a piano concert by Alice Herz-Sommerová, playing all the Chopin

Études without a break. Her virtuosity transported listeners from wretched, starving Terezín to a different world and a different epoch. Sitting on that wooden bench, I listened spellbound. It was an unforgettable evening.

Among the inmates were many professional musicians: concert leaders and soloists, composers, singers, and conductors. Karel Ančerl had his little orchestra. Conductor Rafael Schächter assembled another opera chorus and performed *The Bartered Bride* that made the audience cry. There was an outstanding young pianist and composer, Gideon Klein; also Viktor Ullman, professor of musical theory, who wrote a striking modern opera while he was in Terezín: *Císar z Atlantidy, The Emperor of Atlantis.*

This opera had a topical text with a political edge, written by young Peter Kien, which was bound to strike the German censors as provocative. Though rehearsals were completed, it was banned and never saw a performance. But the plot is worth retelling:

An imaginary country is ruled by the cruel emperor Überall, Overall, who wages war against everyone. The slaughter is pitiless. Thousands die. Death himself cannot stand the sight of it any longer and informs the tyrant that he is going on strike. People stop dying and just crawl around with as much strength as they can muster. There are hordes of them, and constantly their numbers increase.

The emperor summons Death and begs him to resume his duties and allow people to die. Death accepts his pleading, but on one condition only—that the dictator is the first to die. End of opera. If only it might have come true.

23. TEREZÍN IS WOUND DOWN

Autumn 1944, and still the war went on. Hope alternated with despair. Even though news filtered through that the German army was retreating before the might of the Russian colossus and Anglo-American air power, all this seemed academic. It had no connection with us. On the contrary, the clouds over Terezín were growing ever darker.

The end came suddenly. Terezín was to be closed, the fate of its inmates thereby sealed for good. The orders read: *5,000 men to report for transport eastwards tomorrow, a further 3,000 the day after.*

The streets were suddenly transformed into rivers of people. All was bustle and excitement. Knots of inmates gathered to discuss the impending changes and to swap guesses. But no one could say where we were all bound or why. The town changed its character overnight, with everyone rushing to collect cases and rucksacks, find food for the journey, deliver last-minute messages. Quick, quick, for tomorrow we go. The transport department became a teeming anthill.

The Germans in charge announced that all they needed at the moment was fit young men to set up another temporary camp. Meanwhile, their families, wives, and children would remain safely in Terezín. It sounded very uncertain, but there was no avoiding their instructions.

My brother came to say a hasty goodbye to my mother, sister, and me, where we had quickly gathered in my mother's billet in Hamburg. The fact that 5,000 men were to go alleviated the sense of *personal* tragedy. In all the rush there was no time for brooding. As a single man my brother was at least spared the worry of those who were parting from wives and children, as so many were—

hugging and kissing them and having no idea whether they would ever see them again.

"Don't worry about me, Mother," he said. "There are plenty of us, we're young and we can stand a lot. Anyway, the war will be over soon; it can't last much longer. I'll send you word if I can. If not, we'll all meet again at home when the war's finished."

We all gave him our bread rations and three strips of margarine for the journey and kissed goodbye. Early the next day he was taken off with the others in sealed cattle cars.

After that the town never recovered its normal mood. Further transports, each 2,500 strong, followed at short intervals. The whole business of running the town was in disarray. With so many able people disappearing from the top positions, an effort had to be made to replace them, but it was no easy task. People still had to be fed, the sick looked after, corpses cremated, and administration maintained. All the name files had to be right so the Germans could check them. Everyone found their workload doubled.

As always, there was no information about where those thousands of men had been sent. Rumors began to circulate that they were not being used to make a new camp at all but had been carted off to a concentration camp called Auschwitz-Birkenau. No further details. The wives who had been left behind waited impatiently for some news, however meager, to come from their husbands. But nothing came. Not a line. Silence.

Amid the ensuing tension came the announcement, virtually an order, that the German High Command in its kindness and humanity was offering all those women whose husbands had been taken away the opportunity to go and join them in the interest of family unity. Those who wished to volunteer for this purpose must do so that very same day.

No one hesitated. They signed up to the last woman. Crowds of women and children besieged the registration department for permission to travel voluntarily in the wake of their menfolk. For the women in the lines standing there until nightfall, the mood was one of joy at the chance to rejoin their husbands.

There were skeptics in the camp who had had clandestine information from outside. "It's all a German trick," they warned, "a scheme for getting helpless people onto the eastward transports with minimum fuss. Don't volunteer and don't take your children! You'll never see your men again anyway!"

But the cynics were dismissed as prophets of doom and no one took their warnings seriously. All the women, with their children, who volunteered to go and join their husbands, even though they were not told where, left two days later. Nothing more was ever heard of them.

The population of Terezín was visibly thinning. No new inbound transports were arriving, while outbound ones were leaving almost daily with thousands of people. None of us now had any illusion of being left here in relative safety. We were just waiting for our turn to come. We didn't have to wait long.

24. AUSCHWITZ-BIRKENAU

October 15, 1944, was a dismal autumn Sunday. Up to then, Sundays had been like any other day; but this one was different. We were summoned on that day to join the eastward transport: a strip of pink paper with your name and number staring you in the face, a simple brief label hiding your fate as though in invisible writing.

A picture flashed through my mind of the country fair in the small town where we had lived before the war, where a parrot took horoscope cards out of a box with its beak for people to see what fate had in store for them. If they didn't like what they read, they could tear up the card and go home. I was holding my fortune in my hand, but it told me nothing about the future. It kept its secret. I couldn't throw it away. I had to take it into the train car with me and wait for destiny to unfold.

My family was all ready for the journey—or rather what remained of my family: Mother, Lidá, and me. My brother had left the week before, Grandmother shortly before that, and Father had already been in prison for four years.

Terezín culture had been dealt a staggering blow. All the actors, directors, musicians, and conductors—all the artistic people—had received their summons to join the transport. Gustav Schorch, director; Franta Zelenka, stage designer; Hans Krása and Viktor Ullman, composers; Gideon Klein, pianist and composer; Raphael Schächter and Karel Ančerl, conductors. These and many others: 1,500 in all.

We were only allowed to take with us the barest necessities.

Germans themselves handled the administration of the transports. Cattle cars were waiting for us on the siding. We stood in the rain all night in a courtyard with our luggage by our sides so as to be ready when our names were called. They counted us over and over again to be sure no one was missing and the figures tallied.

Finally, in the early morning of October 17, we climbed into the cars and moved off, a weird step into the darkness with nothing before one's eyes. Where to? No idea. Only fear and uncertainty remained. The cars were bolted and sealed from the outside. There were no windows. The air was clammy and hard to breathe. Those who could, squeezed onto the few wooden benches; the rest squatted on the floor. We were in for a long and appalling journey. Two buckets served the whole car for sanitation. When nature called and self-control ran out, people had to forget modesty. German rule, we saw, had reduced us to subhuman standards.

There were about 130 of us in our car, including little children who were thirsty and kept crying. The old folks sitting on the floor propped themselves against the sides. Some of them were praying, some had given up hope. Three people in our car died before we reached our destination.

Opposite me sat Raphael Schächter, who had been the prime mover of musical activities in Terezín. Holding his messtin in his hand he took his last bread ration from his knapsack, a tin of sardines (sheer luxury and hard currency in Terezín) from one pocket, and a spoon from the other. He passed the whole lot over to me, and said, "Break the bread into my tin—would you—then open the sardines and mix it all together. It's going to be my last supper."

He said this with the decisive tone of a man going to the gallows who has been allowed one last wish. Why, I wondered, is he giving up now? Has he an inkling of worse to come?

He ate the food with relish, and his last supper it probably was. For suddenly, after twenty-nine endless hours in that train, we saw the station sign through the cracks: AUSCHWITZ-BIRKENAU. The train came to a halt. We had arrived.

As soon as they opened the doors, noise and confusion broke out. Uniformed guards holding dogs on their leashes shouted "*Raus! Raus!*—Out! Out!—and rained down random blows with their truncheons. Not having stood up for more than a day, people's legs gave way when they tried to jump out and they simply collapsed on the ground.

There was no platform where the train had stopped, merely the end of a siding, leading nowhere. It was the end of the journey, then. Was it our end? Who could say?

"*Gepäck im Wagen liegen lassen, nichts mitnehmen!*" screamed the guard. Leave all luggage behind, and make it snappy! "*Raus! Raus! Schnell! Los!*" He used his boot to make his point. I jumped down to help Mother off the train; my sister was already beside me. Most of those around us were terrified and bewildered, like people roused from sleep in the middle of the night, at a loss to know what was going on. But Mother had sized up the situation in her own way and said to us quietly, "We must keep tight hold of each other now, so that we don't get separated." She took my sister's hand.

I took a deep breath of air. It smelled of smoke, with a curious sweetish tang, like scorched meat. I thought there must be a slaughterhouse nearby, where they were burning cattle bones and offal. No other explanation occurred to me.

All around as far as the eye could see were low, narrow, windowless wooden huts, surrounded and separated from each other on all sides by high fences of electrified barbed wire, with tall watch towers at intervals. The ground was covered with deep sticky mud and great puddles of water.

At this point I spotted the first prisoners inside the grounds. They wore striped uniforms with numbered squares on their backs and queer, frightened expressions in their eyes. They went everywhere at a trot, even when carrying heavy loads, they were followed by guards with truncheons who drove them on whenever they slipped in the mud.

On the other side of the railway line, again surrounded by barbed wire, was a women's camp. The inmates at that moment were standing silently in five columns. They were all wearing extraordinarily torn clothes and rags, were either barefoot or shod in huge wooden clogs, and had no hair on their heads. They scarcely looked human, more like creatures from another world.

Who on earth could they be? I wondered. What country have they come from? What are they doing here?

They stood there silently, not moving, but with horror in their eyes. Up and down the columns strode an SS woman guard with a whip. Where on earth was I? What was this place? I had never seen or read about anything like it; no one had prepared us for such a scene—that a place like this could exist. I felt as if I had fallen into some deep abyss and strayed into an unknown, terrifying underworld where devilish powers held sway, and there was no way out.

Suddenly, quite unexpectedly, a revelation shot through me like a flash of lightning that in a hundredth of a second, illuminates the whole night countryside and you see where you are.

The revelation took the form of a voice, from where I didn't know. It spoke to me firmly and distinctly. "Now it will be a matter of bare life. Death reigns supreme here . . . You are in mortal danger, girl . . . but if you are lucky enough not to be killed, you have enough strength in you to survive . . . hard though it will be."

These words calmed me down. I took a deep breath and sensed that someone or something, somewhere, was holding a protective arm over me. My fear fell away.

"Just keep calm," Father had said, when the Gestapo took him away. "Calmness is strength."

At this moment one of the guards roared out a command: *"Vorwärts! Los! Marsch!"*—Move on! Move on!—and started hitting anyone within reach of his truncheon. The conductor Karel Ančerl was in line in front of me, holding in his arms a little boy about a year old who must have been born in Terezín. His wife was next to him. An SS guard pushed between them, snatched the child from him, thrust it into the wife's arms, and gave Karel a kick that sent him sprawling in the mud.

Amid general confusion the crowd moved into marching order. Now without our luggage, Mother, Lidá, and I staggered on for more than a mile, carried along by the human river around us. In the row behind me was a young mother with a curly-haired blond girl of about four. The child held on to her mother with her left hand, while in her right hand she held a doll in a white dress with red polka dots.

"Where are we going to, Mommy?"

"To see Grandmother."

"Grandmother?" crowed the girl. "Oh, good! Is she expecting us?"

"Yes."

"I'm so thirsty, mommy. Will Grandmother have some milk for us?"

"Yes."

"Will we be there soon?"

"Yes, darling. Quite soon." And the girl skipped with delight.

Finally we reached our destination. Three SS officers stood with legs astride at the end of the path in skin-tight uniforms, with skull-and-crossbones emblems on their caps and jackboots polished to a shine like mirrors. They looked sternly ahead. The one in the middle, wearing gloves, was dividing the column in two. He gestured leisurely with his forefinger to each arrival to go left or right. *"Links! Links! Links! Rechts! Links! Links! Rechts!"*

It was a quick process. Within a matter of minutes he had separated 1,500 women, men, and children into two groups, left and right, like a strange fork in the road, with no time for questions or farewells. I could see that the old, the sick, and women with children were being sent to the left; the young and fit to the right. The Ančerls were just in front of me. With one wave of his hand the SS officer split them apart. Karel was directed right, his wife and child left. We did not know that right meant life and left was death. Now it was our turn.

Mother's expression was baleful. I looked the officer in the face. He was a handsome man, not evil looking, though his clear blue eyes had a glint of cold steel.

"*Links,*" he said to my mother without a thought.

And, with the same equanimity, "*Rechts*" to me.

To my sister he said nothing. In a flash I grabbed her arm and pulled her to the right, next to me. I just had time to catch Mother's terrified look. It carried a silent message: *I wonder where you are going? Perhaps I shall never see you again.*

And she was gone, lost in the crowd streaming leftward. Just behind us came the little fair-haired girl with the doll, clutching her mother's hand. "*Links!*" the officer ordered casually.

Until then I felt like a spectator rather than a victim, as if I were watching from outside, detached, while devilish things went on all around me.

Everything had to be done on the double, one-two, one-two. Dusk was falling. A weird sight in the distance caught my eye. A group of women, naked and bald, were trotting in formation out of one of the wooden huts across an empty space lighted by powerful searchlights. Who were they? Where were they running? They didn't look like human beings—more like figures from a waxworks. I was determined to stay clearheaded even if nothing made sense.

Our group, which had been sent right, consisted of some three hundred healthy young women up to thirty-five years of age. A woman SS guard took us over and we doubled into the first wooden barracks. Inside was an empty room where we were ordered to take off all our clothes—underwear, stockings, and shoes included—and leave them in a neat pile until, she assured us, we came back for them later, after we'd had a shower.

So there we stood, stark naked. Jewelry, rings, and watches were to be left with our clothes. I took everything off except the tin ring Arno had given me before he was taken. That, I was resolved never to be separated from. It would remain my source of strength, my hope of reunion, my torch of love. It would keep my heart warm.

We now had to go through a narrow opening in single file to be further inspected by a uniformed SS man, to make sure we had all obeyed orders and were not trying to hide or smuggle anything.

It was nearly my turn when we heard cries and entreaties, blows, and confusion. One of the girls had tried to conceal an engagement ring under her tongue and the SS man had found it. She was beaten up and taken away. The girl in front of me noticed I still had my ring on. "For Christ's sake take that thing off. You must be mad! He'll kill you. And just for a piece of tin that's not worth a cracker? You saw what he did to the girl in front of us!"

Only a piece of tin, as she put it. But it was all I had and I wasn't going to throw it away. It would be like betraying Arno and saying I didn't care what became of him. The ring was our bond.

I started moving backward in the file to give myself time to think.

Was the other girl right or was I?

Throw it away or keep it?

If I throw it away, I thought, I will have deserted Arno in my own eyes and lost the moral ground under my feet.

If I keep it, the SS man may find it or may not. It was like Russian roulette. Perhaps my life was now at stake. My mind was made up. I decided I must keep the ring, since all my love and hope rested with it.

For better or worse, I slipped it under my tongue, just like the other girl.

I stepped in front of the SS man, knowing full well what I was doing and what risk I ran but prepared to pay the price. I put my life on the line. He started ruffling through my hair to see what he could find. I was expecting him next to tell me to open my mouth.

At that moment, an order rang out from his superior to speed up the inspection. With a push he sent me on my way.

"Next one! Hurry up!"

The ring stayed with me.

It had been my first test in facing up to my destiny, and I felt I had passed. The fact that I had saved the ring filled me with fresh confidence that I had nothing to be afraid of.

In the next room was a long wooden bench. About ten male guards were sitting on it, all with clippers in their hands. Each of us had to go up to the "barber" and have all the hair shaved from her body—long and short, from the head, armpits, crotch—everywhere.

We were standing up to our knees in piles of hair. Brown, blonde, black, auburn, straight, curly. We were changed beyond recognition. My sister stood next to me, her eyes shining from beneath her bald scalp. We stared at each other in amazement for a while, recognizing each other only by our voices.

When the last of us had been shaved we were chased into a kind of rotunda with three tiers of benches all around up to the ceiling. Instinct urged me to run to the very top so that I could have an overall view. The room quickly filled up with naked, shorn, women, sitting motionless, packed closely together, wild-eyed. An eerie sight it was, like a collection of bald mannequins waiting for their wigs and clothes before being arranged in a window display.

Suddenly, a new order: *"Alle heraus!"* We were herded out into a large concrete basement "for a shower." There were scores of women at the door from another transport that had just joined us. Most of them were Hungarians. They insisted they had information that had never reached us in Terezín. These were not showers at all, they said, but gas sprays, and we were all going to be asphyxiated.

"Everyone inside, get on with you!" the guards shouted, and a dozen or so of them started to push us in.

The Hungarian women fought, screamed, and tried to get out, but it was useless; they were squeezed in by brute force. The steel doors were bolted behind us.

The whole ceiling was crisscrossed with a grid of metal pipes with a shower head at each junction. Was it for water or for gas? What would be the point of spraying us with gas? I reasoned. Nonsense. We had been told we were going to have showers, and that was that. I held my sister close beside me, both of us under a shower head.

Suddenly we felt a spray of hot water. I knew I had been right. The Hungarians had only been panicking.

There was no soap, just water. The flow stopped, the steel doors opened, and women guards moved in to drive us out again—*"Alle heraus! Schnell! Los! Heraus! Heraus!"* cracking their whips.

Wet and scalded, we emerged into the cold October night and ran on the double from one block to another across brightly lighted courtyards.

My God! Now I recognized the group of naked, hairless, waxwork women I had been so puzzled by a few hours before. Now I knew. It was us, and all those who were to come after us.

We were chased into a kind of drafty barn, lined up in fives, close together. It was not exactly my aim ever to be in the front row. I shifted to be the last in a row and to be as inconspicuous as possible. At that moment I became aware that nature, heedless of the situation, was asserting itself. A trickle of blood was running down my leg. How pleased I was that there was a tall girl in front of me so the guard couldn't see me. But my luck didn't hold. The woman guard returned to inspect our row. She noticed that I was almost hidden at the far end and shouted "You there!" and pointed at me. "Move forward, quick!"

I moved up, and as soon as she saw the blood all hell broke loose.

"*Du Schwein! Du jüdische Sau!* she screamed, in a fit of rage. She pulled the whip out of her jackboot with the lead ball at its end, bellowing like an insane thing, and started lashing me across the breasts.

The weapon drew blood. Now there was red everywhere. I flinched slightly, turning my head, but then stood like a marble statue, afraid that she would kill me if I tried to fend off her blows.

At this moment a tall thin SS woman came in and ordered her to move us into the "clothing room." That brought the guard's fit of rage to a halt and saved me. Since she had to defer to higher authority, she stuck the whip back into her boot and shouted at us to get out.

Once more we ran on the double into another barracks, a line of bloody drops marking my trail. At the back of the hall were two great piles of motley clothing, no better than rags, plus another pile of assorted shoes. A guard was standing over each pile.

As we ran past, a guard threw to us, at random, whatever she happened to pick up from the pile. That was what we wore from then on. We had to catch it as we ran out of the barracks. Not until we got outside could I stop to look at what I had been given. I found myself holding an olive green georgette evening gown with pearls all over and flashing sequins around a deep-cut neck. Its size was undefined—full of loose ends and trailing sleeves with more gaudy decoration.

In addition, I had been thrown a jacket to fit a twelve-year-old, blue with red stripes and a blue lining. Also a pair of socks, one short and green, the other longer and purple. In my other hand I held a pair of men's black patent leather shoes, big enough to fit a giant.

Shivering in the cold, I quickly put everything on. The sky above was already full of stars. The piles of clothes had obviously been leftovers from the confiscated baggage of the various transports as they arrived. Who, I wondered, could have been the owner of the green gown I was now wearing? Why did she bring it here? To what sort of place did she imagine she was going? It had a nineteenth-century look and could have been worn in a stage play about society ladies who dressed for dinner. Now I would be wearing it in another sort of play, with a very different setting and plot.

I threw the jacket over my shoulders and slid into the outsized shoes. Since they kept falling off I quickly squashed down the backs and flopped around in them like huge slippers, so as not to lose them. Some of the girls had been given heavy wooden clogs.

Outfitted this way, we finally reached the quarters assigned to us. It was one of the long, narrow, windowless shacks that I had seen when we arrived. There were rows and rows of them, all identical. The inside suggested a vast barn divided in half by a red brick stovepipe running up the middle of the floor. It was like a demarcation line separating left from right. I doubt whether it was ever intended to keep the shack warm. It was bitterly cold inside.

The space was filled with three tiers of bunks close together. The lowest almost on the ground, the middle one close above, the top tier only just shy of the ceiling. There were no single beds.

About ten people had to squeeze together like sardines on each bunk. There was only room to sit hunched up. Since we couldn't move, we simply lay there ten to a bunk, with no cover, waiting to see what would happen next.

We immediately formed groups of similar age and interests, girls who had known one another from Terezín. In addition to my sister Lidá, whom I now kept tight hold of, our five included my old friend Marta. Miraculously, she had been drafted into our transport with Dr. Karel Bloch, her husband; Nana Krásová, wife of the composer Hans Krása, who had delighted Terezín with the children's opera *Brundibár,* and Anita Kohn, wife of the well known oboist, Pavel Kohn, were also there. He, as we learned a few days later, had been drafted into the camp orchestra as soon as he arrived. This orchestra had to play the prisoners to work each morning, and accompany them with classical music each evening as they arrived back exhausted, or, often enough, dead.

We felt sure the five of us could help one another. If one stumbled, the others would lend her moral support and keep her head above water. There would be complete mutual reliance, come what might. Those of our fellow inmates who now found themselves among total strangers were in a worse plight. Nothing more happened that first night. We were cold, hungry, and thirsty. We were given neither food nor water. In the end, worn out by the journey and by everything that had happened to us here on our first day, we simply fell asleep from exhaustion.

But before dropping off, I tore a thin strip from the lining of my jacket, threaded it through Arno's ring, and hung it securely where it could not be seen under my evening gown.

I glanced down at my row of nine bedfellows, seeing them now for what they were—bald, bizarrely clad creatures behind the barbed wire fence I saw when we arrived. Their shorn heads were like so many skulls tossed into a pile, one much like another.

Where on earth had we ended up? In what unimaginably strange place? Our outward transformation had taken no time at all. But our invisible inner strength, our moral and spiritual balance, that was something we had to keep firm and inviolate, no matter what twists of fate awaited us.

My thoughts went to each member of my family. Mother was no doubt in some other shed not far away. Who knew if my father and brother might not be in the same camp too, all unaware. What joy it would be to catch sight of one of them, even through barbed wire.

Finally I fell asleep with the others on the hard wooden planks, in my evening theater wear and men's patent leather shoes. And so our first night in Auschwitz passed, leaving us blissfully ignorant of the secret happenings yet to be revealed.

At five in the morning the imperious voice of the SS woman in command burst out, *"Alle heraus! Zählappell! Raus! Raus,"* as she cracked her whip in the air. Roll call. We jumped down half asleep and out onto a huge parade ground. Immediately we had to form up in fives. It was still dark except for a few dim stars.

The counting began. 5, 10, 15, 20, on and on. There were about three hundred of us. After checking our numbers again, the SS woman simply walked off. We had been told not to move or say a word. We stood there like soldiers on duty, silent and motionless for about three hours. When she finally returned she recounted us and shouted the next order: *"Alle ins Waschraum! Los!"* All into the washroom! Run!

The "washroom" was another huge barn with a concrete trough running all around the wall and a water pipe over it with taps at three-foot intervals. Water dripped rather than flowed from them. We all rushed to the taps, pushing and shouting to get to the water. It became impossible to get near the taps. Those who were nearest drank what they could get. No one dreamt of washing. I finally managed to get my hand through the crowd under a tap and swallow a handful before the SS woman returned and ordered us on parade for yet another roll call.

"*Five, ten, fifteen, twenty!*" she shouted, and then left us standing for two more hours. Still no food, and nothing to drink but the few drops I had managed to snatch in the washroom.

The sky became overcast and rain began to fall. We kept on standing. The SS woman went off and came back in a raincoat. We had to stay still, soaked to the bone. If anybody caught a chill, they caught a chill. There was no avoiding it.

It was nearly midday before someone came to check the numbers once more and chase us back into our shack. We were told that two prisoners could volunteer to be block leaders, responsible for keeping watch over us and dividing out the bread rations. About 150 women frantically thrust up their hands, mostly Poles and Hungarians. Not a single Czech. We refrained from offering cooperation, even though we knew it would put us at the mercy of the new powers-to-be.

Finally a cauldron of soup arrived, the first food we had tasted since leaving Terezín. It seemed like ten years ago rather than three days. Terezín had meanwhile disappeared from our consciousness as if it had never existed.

Our two block leaders, Hungarians, immediately started distributing the soup. One full tin between five, who took turns slurping it up. There were a few cabbage leaves swimming in it, which you had to fish out with your fingers. There were no spoons. It was obvious that the leaders were keeping the biggest helpings for themselves and their friends.

We squeezed back onto our bunk, sitting like hunchbacks and wondering what the next surprise would be. In this place nothing could be foreseen.

Three male prisoners came in. One of them I instantly recognized as Ota Weil. He had helped us with the theater lighting in

Terezín, but had left two years ago. So now we knew where they had all been sent.

All three men were working in the camp as electricians and were able to move about freely. Ota had come to see if his sister was among us. I jumped down right away to greet my old colleague. But though he recognized me he looked different now, with a strange, absent expression in his eyes like a man from another world.

"When did you get here?" he asked.

"Sometime yesterday afternoon."

"Alone?"

"No, my sister's here with me. And Mother."

"Your mother's still with you, or did she go to the left?"

"She went to the left. I suppose she's in another barracks with older women."

He took me to the door, opened it halfway, and pointed to a column of red flames rising high up to the sky from a nearby tall chimney. "That's where she went," he remarked dryly. "She went up the chimney."

What was he babbling about? Poor Ota, he'd been here two years and all the things he'd seen and experienced here must have driven him crazy. I suddenly felt sorry for him and to avoid further argument said, "Yes, I suppose so."

I had seen the flames, sure enough, but had persuaded myself it must be a bakery. To feed so many mouths they no doubt had to bake bread nonstop, right through the night. Realizing I was not going to see eye-to-eye with Ota, I bade him a quick farewell. I was a new arrival, still in full possession of my senses, whereas he, poor guy, was not.

"Everyone who went to the left was sent straight up the chimney," he added, as we said goodbye.

· · ·

Time passed. Each day was like the others. We were either lying on our bunks or standing outside. Hour after hour we stood in the rain, in the mud, in puddles, or wherever. If the guard was in a good mood she would hiss through her teeth *"Five, ten, fifteen, twenty, ninety-five, one hundred"* and leave it at that. But if she had had a bad day she would cheerfully make us kneel in the mud or stand for a few hours longer.

On one occasion she announced we were going to get tattooed the next day. Everyone was to get a number. Not on our forearm, as we had seen on prisoners that had been here a long time, but on our forehead.

We waited helplessly for the operation to begin, but nothing happened. A twist of fate had intervened and we were never tattooed. They had run out of ink.

Our dismal camp life dragged on. We slowly forgot normal outside existence: woods, nature, and the setting sun; birdsong and forest murmurs, the bustle of the streets. We lost the very concept of time. The memories of home life became a kind of odd dream.

It seemed unreal that in other places there were people sitting down to supper at this hour, whole families together, then sleeping in their own beds and each going their own way the next morning. Reality was what surrounded us here in the camp. This was the only truth, the only matter that concerned us. Everything else was illusion.

From time to time rumors circulated. Where they came from and who passed them on was a mystery. They traveled along the grapevine. We heard them all, but many made no sense to us. One report was that a truck with a black tarpaulin cover was going around the camp and that whichever barracks it stopped in front of, all the inmates had to get in and were driven straight to the gas chamber. We refused to believe this, but we felt instinctively that devilish things were going on behind our backs about which we knew nothing.

Standing on the parade ground, we often saw white windowless ambulances going past with large red crosses painted on each side. If there were Red Cross vehicles around, we reasoned, they must be bringing first aid materials and medicines for the sick.

Cynics maintained that all they were delivering was gas for killing people. This we obstinately refused to believe.

One day I confronted a particularly dangerous situation.

We were chatting as usual on our bunk just under the ceiling when I saw an old Terezín friend whom I had not noticed before sitting on the other side. I decided to visit her by crawling from one top bunk to the next across the narrow gangway. Suddenly I saw an SS man standing right below. He looked up at me and bellowed for me to get down: *"Runter!"*

I jumped down in front of him, and he eyed me carefully from head to foot.

"Du kommst mit!"—you come with me!—he ordered. As I followed him to the door, I sensed that the dice had fallen and there was no point in resisting. I saw the horror in everyone's eyes. They were convinced they were seeing the last of me.

I had no specific fears, since I had no idea what to be afraid of. Outside the barracks there was no one around. We went along empty lanes between barbed-wire fences. The guards on the lookout tower saw us and waved us by. Finally we came to a block just like ours. The officer opened the door and pushed me inside. It was completely empty, not even a bunk in sight, just a square red brick stovepipe running along the floor from end to end. I noticed piles of objects strewn along it. I took a step closer to see better what they were. Surgical instruments.

My first idea was that he was going to kill me. I could only pray that it would be over quickly. I am completely in his power, I thought, and nothing and nobody in the world can save me. I sought comfort in fate. Consigning myself to God's hands I felt a little better. *"Ausziehen und niederlegen"*—Undress and lie down, came the command.

But the next development was not what I had been expecting. The officer simply stuck a large needle into a vein on my arm and told me to keep pumping my fist. That was all he wanted. My blood flowed plentifully. I thought I might bleed to death and stopped pumping.

"Weiter mache!"—Just carry on!—he insisted, and slapped me across my face.

When he had filled all the containers he had with my blood he pricked my earlobe, presumably to get a blood-type sample, and ordered me to go out quickly. *"Heraus! Und schnell! Los!"*

Throwing on my evening dress and patent leather shoes I raced from the block. But now there was a new danger, for I was completely alone. Leaving a block unaccompanied was strictly forbidden. Anyone trying to escape was shot immediately. What if the sentry saw me? He would shoot me without a second thought. The best thing would be to walk slowly so as not to suggest any intention of escape. The route along the empty path seemed endless, the silence total. There was no sign of life anywhere. No one saw me, until I finally recognized our barracks and crawled inside. When the new block leader saw me she threw a fit, yelling and hitting me: "Where have you been? How dare you? We'll all be shot because of you!"

She carried on like she was demented. Coming back had shaken me more than leaving it, but I climbed up quickly to the top bunk. Everybody was relieved and happy to see me back. My sister wept with joy. They wanted to know exactly where I had been and what had happened. Even though we were sitting doubled up we were at least together, and I suddenly felt safe among these friends, almost at home. Curious how quickly one adapts. But there was no time for long explanations. We were faced with a new situation.

The dreaded black tarpaulin truck had stopped in front of our barracks. Panic arose. A dozen women guards ran in with whips in their hands, with the same number of male guards wielding truncheons. They were evidently prepared to deal with any resistance. Forming two close ranks on either side of the door, they drove us into the vehicle with their shouting. Those who had heard about the truck put up a violent struggle, but in vain. With whips and truncheons they forced us all into the truck too, and then the doors were bolted shut.

We could feel ourselves being driven on a zigzag route through the camp, though we could see nothing. There was chaos inside. "This is the end of us," some of the girls were wailing. "They'll gas us and we'll all be finished!"

Totally ignorant, we had no clear idea what they were talking about. Gas? Gas chambers? These words had hardly entered our vocabulary yet. Finally the vehicle came to a stop and we jumped out. Immediately the word went around that we were standing in front of a gas chamber.

"Form fives, get counted!" We were told to stand there until our turn came. The gas chamber was in use and we had to wait until it was empty. Why pick on our particular barracks? No doubt, said some, because we were unproductive and they wanted to get rid of us.

There we stood, all night and through the following day, fifty-three hours with no food or water. Like people condemned to death—no further need to feed us. With a supreme effort of will, not one of us fainted.

I was not thinking of death, nor did the events of my life unfold before my eyes. I merely felt terribly thirsty and weak after losing so much blood. I felt very tired and had a longing to sit down. I summoned all my strength to stay on my feet and avoid collapsing.

Once again, events took an unexpected turn.

25. EAST TO KURZBACH

Suddenly an order came from on high that a transport of two thousand women, including the thousand of us who were waiting for the gas chamber, was to be organized immediately and sent farther east to dig trenches. Trenches? Where? In defense against whom? Were the Russians getting so close we were supposed to hold them up? Our bare hands against the Soviet army?

Fortune had been kind to us. Strange turns of fate often occurred when we least expected them, even here. Instead of being consigned to the gas chamber, we were now marched off in fives to a railway nearby. There were already many other women there. We were squeezed into a train, a passenger train this time. Soon we began to move. It seemed like a miracle that we should be leaving the horrors of Auschwitz, but the SS guards walking up and down the coaches loudly disabused us of any false hope.

"You'll soon be back again," they sneered. Still, we were on our way to somewhere else, which couldn't be as bad as here, we thought. Experience soon taught us that every change was for the worse, but it is not in human nature to accept this until it is proven to be true.

Each of us was now given a crust of bread for a three-day journey. Starving as we were, we all swallowed the bread immediately without a thought for tomorrow. We were to be in that train, in fact, for about two days and two nights, passing through unfamiliar countryside and villages, farther and farther eastward.

At last the train halted and we got out. Around us were fields and meadows that none of us recognized.

The grapevine, however, was busy as usual, and we discovered we were in Upper Silesia, at a lonely spot called Kurzbach, not far from Breslau. It was already November. Along the road, the trees were leafless, the ground muddy, and the sky gray with heavy clouds. A sharp breeze blew up. It started to drizzle. We were soon shivering with cold.

After a march of several hours we reached our destination. It seemed to be some kind of farm, of which only two huge wooden barns remained. One stood beside the main road, the other on a slope on the opposite side.

They assigned as many of us as possible to one or the other barn; my group was put in the higher one. The overflow, some fifty women, were housed in a stable with room for ten horses. All three buildings were of thin timber with no windows. A thousand women would stay here, we were told, and the rest would be sent farther on.

The German guards in charge of us were relatively old, either demobilized servicemen or soldiers transferred to the reserve, all in uniform with rifles over their shoulders. There were also two women guards and the camp commander, who were billeted elsewhere. They had a cabin put up for them by the roadside which served as a unit headquarters from which daily orders were issued.

When we walked into our block we found it was lined with the familiar three-tier bunks, long shelves of boards on which ten had to sleep in a row, tightly together. Our five immediately secured a place under the ceiling, which was fairly high and left enough room for sitting up—an unexpected luxury.

On our arrival we were given no food or water. We were soaked to the skin from the rain and freezing from the cold. Worn out, we simply fell asleep on the bare planks. We were allowed to use a latrine that had been dug for us outside the block. I ventured out. It was a dark, starless night and the rain had stopped. My wet clothes clung to my shivering body. When I returned to the barn it looked to me like a vast warehouse with silent human forms laid out on the shelves—perhaps not even particularly human, more like piles of wet rags heaped up at random.

They woke us at five in the morning and immediately had us line up for the numbers check. Then we were split into ten squads, given one spade each, and marched to the site where we were supposed to dig trenches. We were a bizarre bunch, I in my thin green georgette evening gown with all the pearls and shiny beads on it, men's patent leather shoes, bald-headed, and a spade over my shoulder.

At the place where we stopped there was nothing to be seen far and wide, only a bare, flat, treeless wilderness with no feature to rest the eye on. To find ourselves outside in the country, though, with no barbed wire in sight, did give us a slight illusion of freedom. Here, we thought, we can at least breathe fresh air. A little physical exercise won't harm us and might strengthen us. There are no Auschwitz chimneys to threaten us, and none of the elderly guards here was exactly frightening. Who knows? Our labor might even earn us a little more food.

Anyway, the war is bound to end soon. The Russian army is near, almost at the door, so we just have to hold out for a little longer and peace will break out. There will be rejoicing and we will all go back to our various homes. Arno will find me, as promised, whistle our Dvořák theme, and a happy new life will begin. A sudden wave of optimism rose among us; our mood was almost jolly.

But the smiles soon left our faces. We were faced with a new enemy now, one very hard to cope with. We had not yet realized that in this flat, unsheltered region of Silesia the wind blows like an icy whip. Here we were, practically barefoot, close-shaven, and wearing thin rags. The weather soon made itself felt.

There was still frost on the ground when we rose for roll call at five and were given nothing to eat. They led us a couple of miles to the area where we were meant to dig trenches. Did they imagine a few girls, hardly able to lift a shovel, were going to put up effective barriers against the Russian army? The soil was so hard you couldn't drive a pitchfork into it. Our spades merely bounced off.

We stood helplessly not knowing what to do. True, they didn't exactly hound us or check our work, but even standing still for ten hours in a bitter wind with no food was an ordeal. We reached the work site at seven o'clock each morning. After we had stood around for two hours a morning train would pass and whistle every day at the same spot. That meant it was nine o'clock. Our timetable for the day: eight more hours to go.

Limbs shaking and teeth chattering, we huddled into little knots to get some protection from the unrelenting wind. At five in the evening we shouldered our spades and marched back to camp, where we were given a tin full of watery soup.

Twice a week we received a small piece of bread as a three-day ration. It was interesting to see the different ways human nature revealed itself. Someone had found a knife in the barn, a great treasure that we shared among us. One girl would cut her portion into three equal pieces, eat one right away and save the others for the next two days. Another would slit each third into thin wafers to give herself the illusion that she had five slices for supper instead of just one. One girl cut her slices into little squares, another into triangles, and both counted anxiously to see how many fragments she now had per slice. Saving up your bread exposed you to the danger of night time robbery. Yes, some were desperate enough to steal.

I had my own solution. I was hungry. Keeping and guarding the ration over three days was risky. One wretched slice would neither save nor satisfy me. So I'd eat the whole three-day ration all at once. I'd enjoy one good supper and to hell with the next two days. Those I can survive, if I have the pleasure of recalling one square meal. So I sat down in a corner and swallowed my ration with great gusto, regretting only how hungry my friends were going to be that night, and how anxious about theft.

December came and winter closed in. We still had nothing to shield ourselves with from the cold, and many fell ill. We huddled close together for warmth, waiting all night for daybreak to come; then again, waiting all day to get back to the barn after standing for hours in the frost. We slept in our clothes, which were sometimes wet through, on bare boards with no blankets. Our hands and feet froze during the day and water dripped into our always-damp shoes. We used to stand leaning on our spades with our free hand under our armpit for a little warmth, then change hands, to save our fingers from frostbite.

The unequal struggle against the cold drained our willpower as well as our energy. Morale began to sink. But we did find a way to deceive that other enemy, hunger.

26. IMAGINARY FEASTS, A NEEDLE, AND OTHER WONDERS

The trick was to start "cooking." Merely talking about food became a substitute for food itself. Our group of ten girls decided that each of us would take turns preparing a splendid feast featuring at least five choice courses. The cook of the day had to work out the menu and describe each course down to the last ingredient and provide recipes for every item. The scheme worked.

Banquets were served up each day that would have been a credit to any grand hotel: from the laying of the table, through all kinds of soups and hors d'oeuvres, both native and foreign, followed by seafood served on scallop shells. Then, after a decent pause, the main course would arrive: meat of all kinds done in every way the cookbooks had ever told. Poultry and game were accompanied by *knedlíky*—Czech dumplings—potatoes, rice, noodles of all shapes and sizes, and every kind of vegetable, all washed down with good wine. The assortment of desserts was mouth-watering. A good cup of coffee and cake with filling—topped with whipped cream, naturally—completed the meal.

And so it went, turn by turn. There were some excellent cooks among us, vying with each other and never scrimping on the ingredients.

One day there was an incident, however. The hostess for the day was just coming to the end of her menu and explaining the recipe for a festive "Libuše cake."

"This is how we made it in our family," she said. "Blend together a pound of butter, eight dessert spoonfuls of icing sugar, and ten egg yolks, and—"

Don't talk nonsense!" broke in a girl who had lived next door in their home town. "Your mother would never have dreamed of putting ten yolks into any kind of cake batter. She was very tight with eggs and would have used two at the most. Ten? Never! Look, I used to come to your place, and your cakes were never any good, mainly because of the lack of eggs. Goodness knows why she was so stingy. You weren't hard up. So don't boast and don't tell lies." The hostess of the day went red in the face and, not knowing how else to defend her honor, attacked her friend physically. They couldn't tear each other's hair out, as they didn't have any, so they pulled each other to the ground in a fight. We had to separate them forcibly until they calmed down.

We also managed to defeat the bitter cold to a certain extent. One of the inmates in our barn was chosen as a housekeeper for the woman SS guard in command. Instead of standing all day with a shovel like the rest of us, she could stay warm with her new employer. One night she returned to the barn with an unimagined treasure prized above gold—a needle. This needle became our salvation. We agreed that each of us should have it for one evening. And we started sewing. What did we not achieve with that one needle!

We had no proper thread, so we pulled strands out of the clothes we had on. I made a head scarf out of my jacket lining and still had enough material left over to cover my hands with lace-up gloves. Now my fingers didn't freeze so badly. Each of us managed to improve her clothing somehow, especially by way of protecting the head and hands. We treasured that needle and would have given our lives for it.

By another miracle, each of us was issued a blanket. Not a soft, warm, woolly one but only a thin rag of man-made fiber. Still, it was something, and we wrapped ourselves in our blankets like cocoons.

One day as we walked back along the main road from work, one of the local peasant women was coming our way in her warm shaggy coat and high felt boots, a thick shawl around her head and neck and knitted woolen gloves. She had a full pack on her shoulder. When she saw us in our wretched rags, legs all raw from the frost, she stopped, opened her pack, and threw us a pair of long thick stockings. Black, they were. I happened to be nearest to her and caught them with my free hand. I muttered "Thank you," though I could have hugged her and kissed her hand. It was a wonderful present and so unexpected. We could hardly get over the shock.

When we got back to the barn each of the five of us took turns putting them on for at least half an hour. We were a close knit group: my sister Lída, my good friend Marta Blochová, Nana Krásová, Anita Kohnová, and myself. We decided that each of us in turn should wear the stockings for a whole day. And since it was I who had been instrumental in bringing the stockings into the gang, it was decided that I should go first. Heavy snow fell that night and all the next day. And there I was in the morning, stepping out in long woolen stockings. What comfort, what luxury! Along with my evening gown, a blue kerchief over my head now from the jacket lining, and something over my hands too, I felt fully equipped against the extreme cold.

But the winter got no milder. On the contrary, the night frosts became more intense and we had long icicles hanging from the ceiling right above our heads. As more and more of us fell sick, the camp commanders must have reasoned that we would all freeze to death unless something was done. And so we were given sleeping bags—not real sleeping bags, but ordinary paper sacks for potatoes. At least they were big and long enough to climb into. They didn't keep you very warm, but at least they were another layer to help keep away frostbite.

Nana Krásová often lay next to me, a tall beauty who looked like a pale fairy, with great thoughtful eyes. At one time she had had long black hair. She told me she had tuberculosis, but we still used the same spoon for eating our soup. Nana was a clairvoyant. One night I awoke to see her sitting up in her potato sack and staring into the darkness.

"Are you all right?" I asked.

"Yes, perfectly. Only I had a strange dream."

"What did you dream about?"

"I dreamed that Anita and you and I were all in Prague."

"Seems like a rather nice dream."

"Far from it. Anita and I were swimming in the Vltava River, and the current pulled us away from the bank. You were standing on the Charles Bridge, looking all around. You know, Zdenka," she went on, in a perfectly self-assured, matter-of-fact tone, "you're going to be the only one of us left alive. Anita and I will never return home."

Winter advanced. It was nearly Christmas. The countryside lay under deep snow and digging was impossible. Perhaps they'll let us stay in the barns all day, we thought. But while in the normal world people were making Yuletide preparations, baking Christmas cakes, wrapping up candies, and packing presents, here in our world a new ordeal awaited us. Instead of shoveling earth, the order came that we were to carry logs to a sawmill. Our dreams of spending the rest of the winter in our barn melted like snowflakes in our hands.

The new project began immediately. Up at five, roll call, and off on a long march to a forest where timber was stacked in a large pile. Each group of five women had to lift a trunk, rest it on their shoulders and march off with it. *Marsch! Aufgehen! Los!*" shouted the new guard in charge of us. We quickly spaced ourselves at equal distances under each trunk so the load was fairly distributed. There were no proper paths in the woods, and we kept falling into snowdrifts and tripping over roots. Those who only had clogs on their feet found the snow sticking to them and their ankles continually giving way.

The logs on our shoulders got heavier and heavier, but we were not allowed to lay them down for even an occasional rest. *"Marsch!"* the cry would come from the guard on duty, who seemed forever itching to clout us with the rifle he carried on his shoulder.

At last we emerged from the forest onto the highway, where at least we were safe from tripping and could keep the log properly in place on our shoulders. As a former Sokol gymnast, I saw there was only one thing to do.

"Girls," I said, "look. If we want to make it easier for ourselves, we must keep in step and all march in the same rhythm. Let's sing in time." So we started up the old Czech jingle. *One—two—four horses in the yard, no one taking them to plow . . . trala-lalala, trala-lalala.*

"Sehr gut,"—very good, said the guard approvingly.

After another few miles we got to the sawmill. There we could drop our logs to the ground alongside the others. Our knees were knocking and we could hardly stand upright. Each of us got a small tin of thin soup for her efforts. That was our food for the day. When we returned to our barn that evening we collapsed on the bunks out of sheer exhaustion.

Our shoulders were already raw and bleeding; how long could we hold out? This was work for horses, not for half-starved girls whose health and strength were fast running out. We were covering seven miles a day. Every evening we applied snow to our sores, but they were still weeping when we got up. Each day one or another of us collapsed with a high temperature and was sent to the "sick bay," a dark, grubby hole where no one looked after you. There were no drugs or medicine. You either recovered or died.

Our condition was deteriorating rapidly. Marta was the first of our five to go under. She was moved to sick bay and we all said goodbye to her in our hearts. But we took turns going after work to visit her to try to keep her spirits up. "The war can't last long," we said. "Just force yourself to keep going until it's over."

One day something wondrous happened. We were walking home from work. I was last in line as usual. I always tried to be inconspicuous and never pushed myself forward to earn favor. We had a replacement guard in charge of us that day, an older man who might have been a schoolteacher in civilian life. He walked slowly and seemed as tired as the rest of us. He carried the usual rifle but had a kind, quiet expression, as if he would rather have been sitting by his home fire in his slippers with a cat at his feet than be out here guarding prisoners.

Without warning he turned to me and said softly, "Can I give you something?" He used the polite *Sie* for "you," a rare courtesy. I couldn't imagine what he might want to give me, but not to offend him I whispered back, "Of course, surely."

Putting his hand in his pocket, he drew out a beautiful white crusty roll such as none of us had seen for years. He slipped it across to me, adding apologetically, "A mouse has been at it, though."

On closer inspection he was right. In the middle of the roll was a neatly gnawed-out crater, such as only a mouse can make. In fact, the whole roll was hollow, with just the crust left. Never mind, I thought, the mouse must have been hungry too. I was delighted to have it and could have swallowed it whole as I walked along. But suddenly I thought of Marta, ill and equally hungry in the sick bay. She was worse off than I. I must save the roll for her. A little extra can help a lot.

With a great effort I restrained myself from breaking off just a tiny bit of the crust for myself. Marta, after all, had gotten me off the transport in Terezín and rescued me from certain death. I had to try to repay her.

As soon as we reached the barn I rushed off to find her in the sick bay and give her the roll, the biggest gift I could. She had a high fever and was barely conscious. I told her how I had come by the food and she really appreciated it. But the fever had made her thirsty, she said, and she would rather keep it until morning. She took it and put it down beside her. It turned out all wrong. Someone stole it in the night, and Marta never got any of it.

I was still touched by the guard's kindness. Not every German was a beast and sadist, it seemed. There were decent people among them who had been caught up in the maelstrom of war against their will and could find no way out. We never saw him again. I often thought of him.

Back in the barn I lay down to sleep, little knowing what surprises still awaited me that evening. I had Nana Krásová on my left and my sister on my right, where I could keep a constant eye on her. We had said good night when Lída suddenly sat up. "There's something I must tell you," she said.

"Can't it wait until tomorrow?" I asked, thinking it would be something trivial like a complaint about one of the other girls.

"No, I must tell you now."

"Very well, then," I said casually, not giving her words much importance. But she dropped a bombshell.

"I'm pregnant." Silence.

I gasped. "You? Pregnant? For Christ's sake, what else do we need? How on earth did it happen?" She was just sixteen years old.

"Do you remember," she faltered, "those two transports of young men who left Terezín in September? Jirka was in one of them and my friend Petr in the other. Petr and I were very fond of each other and wanted to have a proper farewell. A friend of his lent us his attic room, and that's where it happened. It was my first time. We promised we'd get together again after the war. And the next day Petr was gone."

"Not possible! This is disastrous! Pregnant in this place? With no proper food? And hard labor? And no medical help? How is this going to end up?"

"I don't know. Perhaps the war will be over soon."

"If it started in September, and now it's December, this means you're three months along. So you might give birth in June? Supposing someone notices before then? You remember at Auschwitz how all the pregnant women were sent to the left? God knows what became of them. The main thing now is to keep it absolutely secret. Not a living soul must know except us. God almighty! How am I going to protect you now?"

It was a nightmare. I started watching Lída closely. I was six years older. She was as thin as a rake, but her belly was already bulging a little. I could only pray that no one would notice her condition. Our rations were so meager that the few spoonfuls I could spare of my own soup only helped a little. A worse problem was the strain of carrying those tree trunks several miles to the mill each day. To make it easier for her, I took up the end position with her just in front of me. The timber hardly touched her and the main weight fell on my shoulder.

Time moved on inexorably. It was now January 1945, and still there was no change on the horizon.

One night Nana Krásová suddenly sat up in bed again, woke me up, and said with a serene smile, "You can't imagine what a lovely dream I've had."

"About Prague again?"

"No. This time I dreamed I was standing in the middle of a lovely green meadow, when up trotted a bunch of white horses, twenty-one of them. My Hans was sitting on one. He smiled and motioned to me to get into the saddle with him. I climbed up and we rode off together into the distance. He told me that where we were going to there would be plenty of everything."

"Do you think this dream means anything for the future?"

"Yes. But nothing good. Not yet."

"Why? It was a beautiful dream."

"Zdenko," she said, in her prophetic style, "we will see big changes on the twenty-first of this month. Changes for the worse."

And then she just stopped talking.

27. DEATH MARCH

I had some confidence in Nana's predictions and was curious in the back of my mind to see what would happen on the twenty-first. But it was a day like any other. Roll call at five, march to the woods, haul logs to the sawmill. We didn't even feel like singing on the march, since that, too, used up energy. We gulped down our tins of thin soup and slogged back to the barn, looking forward to finding our plank bunks, crawling into our paper sacks, and shutting our eyes. Then we could forget the cold and hunger and thank God for letting us survive another day.

But it was not to be like that at all.

Having been counted several times over at evening parade, we were expecting to be released when the Lagerkommandant, whom we had rarely seen, appeared before us with official orders.

"Kurzbach has to be evacuated. Those in the sick bay will stay behind, the rest of you will line up here and march off this evening—in one hour's time."

Nana was right. The worst was still to come. So far we had seen and experienced nothing. We went back to our barns but had nothing to pack for our next journey. I did stuff a little straw into my shoes for fear they would fall off. God alone knew where we would have to march and how long it would take.

Suddenly Blanka Krausová, a strong courageous girl who was a distant relation of mine from Prague, came bounding in and shouted breathlessly, "Girls, there's a cellar full of potatoes around the corner. Hurry up and get some for the journey!"

There were indeed potatoes galore. Each of us took as many as she could and stuffed them wherever we found room, into our sleeves or under our clothes, tying string around them so they wouldn't drop out. These potatoes were our only luggage.

Then there was Marta in sick bay. Hadn't the Lagerkommandant said all sick cases would be left behind? What would happen to them? Feverish debate ensued, but there was no time to waste; we decided unanimously not to leave Marta behind.

We ran to the sick bay and dragged her out, fever and all. She had heard nothing. No one had told those inside that the camp was being evacuated. She could hardly stand, but we managed to persuade her it was out of the question to stay. She must summon her last reserves of strength and march with us. We were given a final three-day bread ration made with some kind of bran, all black and moldy. When you are hungry you can eat anything.

We set off, marching in fives through the frosty night. We were accompanied by an unusual number of uniformed German guards with rifles. We had not gone far before we heard violent shouts and screams from the women still locked up in the sick bay, followed by rifle shots. They had shot every patient.

A deathly silence spread over the countryside.

The Russian army was closer now, rapidly advancing westward. The Germans were determined that we prisoners, witnesses to Nazi crimes, should not fall into Russian hands at any price. So they were driving us west ahead of the Russians, deep into German territory. We had landed in an active area of the front and could hear gunfire and explosions echoing day and night. It was music to our ears, for we were confident the Russians would catch up to us any day now, perhaps any hour.

We had to keep marching day and night.

We were overtaken on the road by trucks crammed full of migrating humanity, as the villages in the area were evacuated. People were leaving their homes in haste, often bringing their cattle and poultry with them. The roads were congested with vans and covered wagons. Everyone was in flight, taking whatever he could manage in the hope of saving his life. In the general haste whole towns were soon on the move with the powerful Russian army at their heels.

For three days we had neither food nor sleep. The pilgrimage was becoming a gruesome Calvary. We envied the refugees their canvas-covered wagons, which protected them from the wind and snow, and their ability to sit up or even lie down.

The potatoes we had hoarded began to weigh us down like stones. Now and again we ate one raw for the juice and starch, and it did stave off some of our hunger. A Prague milliner, Mitzi Poláčková, was in the row behind me. She had not taken any potatoes with her. Now she tapped me apologetically on the shoulder.

"Zdenka, excuse me. Do you think you could lend me a few potatoes? I'll return them to you after the war."

I gave her what I could spare. Goodness knows whether they were of any help. In the end they became so heavy a burden we had to get rid of them. With heavy hearts we dropped them on the roadside.

Lack of sleep was a far worse problem. We were at the point of collapse after three days and nights of continuous movement with temperatures dropped below what we thought we could withstand. Breathing was difficult and our noses were transformed into frozen white icicles.

Our very despair produced an idea that saved us. We discovered it was possible to sleep on the march. Nature is merciful. Whoever's turn it was to take a nap would move to the middle of our five, so that those on each side could take her arms and steer her. Sensing this support, the one in the center could nod off, while her legs were moving automatically. She could sleep for at least two hours like this and get over the deadly exhaustion for a while. We all took turns benefiting from this brainchild.

Nevertheless, our ranks were starting to thin out. The weaker ones could not keep pace and gradually fell back, which was fatal.

Anyone who got out of file and fell exhausted in the snow by the wayside was shot without mercy by the nearest German. No power on earth could stop the murderous finger on the trigger. Many girls who had been given heavy clogs that slowed them down took them off and marched barefoot in the snow, simply to stay in line and avoid a bullet from the nearest rifle. But by the fifth day not even the strongest of wills could stand up to the hunger, cold, and exhaustion. Women and girls everywhere were dropping into the deep snow to find peaceful white graves.

Fulfilling my worst fears, Lída now began to fail too. She had been dragging herself along like a ghost, hardly able to put one foot in front of the other. Hanging on my shoulder she whispered, "I can't go on anymore. I'll have to stay here. Leave me. You go on."

I could see she could walk no farther. But what now, for God's sake? I couldn't leave my sister—just say goodbye, wait to hear the rifle shot, and march on.

Is death so simple, a light and silent thing like the snowflakes falling around us? Should I also break ranks, stay with her, and be shot as well? No. That I could not allow. Neither solution was acceptable. Lída would have to muster her reserves and march on. Both of us must survive.

Everything inside me was in revolt.

Somewhere inside each of us is a survival kit. We never know where it is, or what is in it, until it opens at the critical moment. It contains no drugs or bandages, just firm instructions about what to do—and the necessary strength to do it. An immense, mysterious strength that we never know we possess wells up from hidden depths, but only in extreme situations when our lives are at stake. We don't understand where it comes from, or by what miracle it helps us to achieve the impossible.

After I had scolded Lída and virtually ordered her to go on walking, she managed to pull herself together. We put her into the center of our five so she could sleep for a while and get over the worst of her fatigue.

At last they found us somewhere to stop for the night. It was a locked barn with straw piled up in several layers. Inside, it was pitch dark and we couldn't see an inch in front of our noses. When they had shoved us all in they locked the door again. There was complete chaos. Pandemonium broke out. There was no room for the hundreds of us to get any sleep. We had to lie across each other, and we got up in the morning as tired as if we had fought a pitched battle.

When we stopped next we came to realize that the best place to sleep was with the cattle. There was always a fight for places in the cow shed. It was luxury to lie there on dirty straw with the smell of milk and animal warmth all around. There was even some light, and if you managed to grab a spot you could stretch out your bruised and weary limbs. A night with animals, I found out, was not the worst thing in the world. It was less risky, in fact, than with people. So we spent our nights among horses, cows, goats, and sheep.

Our numbers, alas, were dwindling. More and more girls ended up in the snowdrifts, their corpses lining the route.

It must have been the tenth day when we got to the bank of the Oder River. In late January, it was flowing fast and furious, with high waves and ice floes in between.

As our column came to a halt the Lagerkommandant suddenly appeared and delivered a mystifying command: *"Wer kann— weiter; wer nicht—bleiben."* We turned the words of this Delphic oracle around in every direction and finally decided that it meant "Whoever has the strength should keep going; whoever hasn't, stays put."

But he never explained. What did "keep going" mean? Where to? How much farther? And what then? And what did "staying put" imply? The Russians were bound to arrive in a day or two. Would the Germans hand us over to them alive or shoot us all as they had shot the stragglers on the march?

Marta, for all her heroic efforts to get this far, was the first of us to decide to stay put. She just could not manage anymore. Many other girls reached the same conclusion. Others weighed the alternatives. Was it better to stay, not knowing whether the Germans would let us be taken alive, or to go on? After about seventy girls had opted to stay I was still undecided.

The Kommandant had said that those who could should keep going. I for one still had the strength, both to carry on and to drag Lída with me. At that time everyone had to make her own choice, knowing best where her own strength lay.

There was no bridge or ferry across the huge river, only open rafts. They loaded on as many of us as the rafts could take without sinking. We were still a large group and stood awash up to our knees in icy water. There was nothing to hold on to, and the strong current tossed the rafts violently from side to side. Scared that we might all drown, we held on to each other, and after swinging crazily between waves and ice floes, we finally reached dry ground on the other side. Only about half of us had survived the journey from Kurzbach. Marta was the first of our five to go missing. What happened to her after our departure we would never know.

We marched on for another four days and felt as if we had crossed half the European continent in the last two weeks. In fact, we covered nearly 270 miles.

Finally, we reached the gates of Gross Rosen concentration camp. The six hundred of us who were left from the original thousand felt glad to have arrived anywhere at all. It hardly mattered that we were behind barbed wire again. How did the saying go? *Times change, and we change with them.* My first impressions were not that bad. There was a bit of nature to be seen with forest all around, and trees have always had a relaxing effect on me. We almost felt safe. The roof over our heads protected us from severe frost, and we no longer had to march anywhere. The authorities did not have their eyes on us here, and we had no duties to carry out. We went for our soup twice a day and otherwise lay around on the floor, where we also slept. There was, of course, twice-a-day roll call.

Gross Rosen was mainly a camp for men. Columns of prisoners went past us every day on their way to the mines, but they were hardly human. In their long striped coats and convict caps they looked like the shadows of men from whom the last drop of life had been squeezed. Their expressionless eyes gazed at us absent-mindedly, as if they no longer quite belonged to this world.

Alive, but dead. Dead, but alive.

Night fell over our new camp. Everything sank into a deep silence, and we relapsed into restless sleep. I sneaked out of the hut, surrounded by dense barbed wire and the silent, clear, frosty night. There was no one around, only the stars winking down at the human race. No, not winking—rather, mocking the folly, vanity, and pettiness of their transitory short-lived presence on the planet. They seemed to be saying how trivial and ridiculous man was, with his wars, his pride, and his silly little victories. Their lives last no longer than a mayfly's, and they have no idea how to spend them. Gaze upon us, said the stars. We alone remain.

28. MAUTHAUSEN

We had been at Gross Rosen barely a week, and hardly warmed ourselves up, when reports suddenly went around that Russian units were near and Gross Rosen was to be evacuated. Its entire population was to set forth again, deep into western Germany, tens of thousands at a time.

With the memory of our last journey, with its horrors and privations still fresh, we were more than anxious. But this time a long railway train was awaiting us. We were delighted that fortune had granted us this tiny piece of luck, never mind that it was a freight train with low, open coal cars. At least we were going to ride, we told ourselves, instead of having to walk. But once again we learned that every change was a change for the worse. This time, it was far worse than we could imagine. We were another step closer to death and annihilation.

We arrived at the siding where the train stood. They told us to climb up quickly and stand in the cars. About ninety of us squeezed into each car. We thought there was no room for a mouse, let alone a human body. How wrong we were.

Another group of women waiting on the station platform were now told to join us. Another forty bodies were jammed into each car, but there are limits to everything; as it was, each of us was standing on one leg, 130 of us packed so tightly we could hardly breathe. Instinct warned me to hold tight to the waist-high rim on the side of the car and not to let go on any account. There lies your salvation, I told myself. Getting squashed among the mass of bodies in the middle would be fatal.

As the train moved off, hysterical cries for help came from those huddled in the center. They could neither stand nor breathe.

For a day and a night the train pushed on through empty German villages. Nowhere was there a sign of life. We stopped at no stations and were given no food or drink. We were so desperately thirsty that when a little snow fell it seemed like manna from heaven. We licked up every flake, wherever it landed. In our enthusiasm we hardly noticed when the snow turned to rain, and in ten minutes we were drenched. With nothing to protect us, our clothes soaked up the water and froze us to the marrow. Shivering in the cold night air and with eyelids drooping from fatigue, we longed for sleep. It was already our third day on the train.

We were thrown from side to side like passengers in a storm-tossed ship, with no room to shift from one leg to the other. Those who no longer had the strength to stand collapsed onto the floor of the car, where the mixture of coal dust and excrement had turned into a sticky, foul-smelling slime. At the first jolt of the train others of us fell on top of them like an avalanche, crushing some to death. We had no choice; no one could help himself, let alone the others. Desperate shouts for help echoed through the empty countryside as our trainload of half-crazed passengers hurtled along.

Every minute another bout of panic arose and more fatalities followed. I lost my balance at one point, when others pushed me. A corpse lay below me. Unable to get back on to my feet, even onto one leg, I spent the night sitting on it. The only place I could put my hand to prop myself up was on the teeth of the corpse's open mouth.

After five days of this hellish journey we came to a halt on a siding where a sign read WEIMAR. Station staff came and opened the sides of the cars. Within a few minutes the whole platform was transformed into a huge scrap heap with corpses piled high in front of each car, tossed out like so much useless human rubbish. And this in Goethe's Weimar, once the symbol of German culture and a high point of civilization. And those of us who remained in the cars? We were happy to have more room. The human will to survive is indomitable—and callous.

But our journey was not finished. We were supposed to be transferred to a train bound for Buchenwald. But at the last moment they discovered Buchenwald was full. So we were to carry on to another place we had never heard of: Mauthausen.

We were half dead anyway and quite indifferent to where we were going next. Another three unbearable days followed, with the usual cold, hunger, thirst and death. At last they did give us something to eat: moldy bread and some sort of cheese. But our mouths were too dry to swallow a bite. We had no saliva left.

The journey seemed to go on endlessly; we feared it would never stop. But stop it did, late on one cold evening in mid-February. It was a little hillside station bearing the simple sign: MAUTHAUSEN.

We were not even sure what part of Europe we were in. Someone thought it was Austria. If so, we had come quite a way. But why the Germans at this point would be pushing us around from one place to another, sometimes by train, sometimes on foot, no one could explain. All we could see was that there were fewer of us each day.

We crawled out of the cars as fast as we could manage—everything always had to be done for the Germans on the double, one-two. We found our limbs had turned as stiff as logs from the journey and gave way as soon as we tried to walk upright. Many of us had lost our shoes in the train and were now trying to trudge barefoot through the mud and snow.

Slowly we could make out, high up on the hill, the thick walls that surrounded the fortress of Mauthausen. White stone walls gleamed ominously through the darkness. With the last of our energy we clambered up the hill. With Marta gone, the four of us still stayed together. I had held my sister Lída close beside me in the train, while Nana and Anita were on the other side. We had been able to see one another over the heads of the rest, but there had been no means of contact through the mass of bodies in between. Now, however, we were together again at the entrance to the fortress. We passed through the great gray stone gate. Our first impression was of meticulous tidiness—and silence, a frightening total silence. The air seemed thick with it. Not a sound could be heard. It was as if the whole camp had some hideous, closely guarded secret to hide. A vague oppression gripped us. Our nerves, always on edge, told us to expect cold steel at our throats at any moment.

We were led into a long, dark, narrow passageway bordered on both sides with huge granite squares.

Someone suddenly seized my neck from behind. I was always last in line and had twisted my head around close to one of the stones.

"Have a good look!" he said with a devilish grin. "Each stone, one head!" It was the SS guard who accompanying our column.

Just what did he mean, "Each stone, one head?" We outsiders had no inkling of what went on here. But a few days later we found our explanation.

Mauthausen was a men's camp. We were the first female transport to be sent there. In addition to a large Jewish contingent, many of the inmates were political prisoners of all nationalities.

Deep down, all around the fortress, were great granite quarries where the prisoners worked. The rocks were first split with dynamite. Then the prisoners had to haul the heavy blocks on their backs up about 180 steps to the workplace. It was a favorite sport of the guards, when a prisoner had reached the topmost step with his last gasp, to give him a kick so that he and his load hurtled down into the depths together. Thousands of prisoners had perished here over the last few years. Now we knew what it meant, one head for each stone.

We were immediately ordered to the showers and the usual speculation began: water or gas? We were past arguing. Water, it had to be water, water, water. We were so parched with thirst. There is nothing more unbearable—far worse than cold or hunger. There is no antidote for thirst. Cold can be overcome by movement for a while, and even hunger can be tricked. But thirst is sheer torture and only water alleviates it.

They turned on the showers. Hot rusty-colored water came down on us. We all stood underneath with mouths wide open, like fish gasping for air. No one thought of washing. We just drank and drank. Saved at last. Then we threw on our dirty, torn rags and ran across the concrete parade ground. They herded us into a brick building and locked the door.

Inside, the rooms were lined with the usual three-tier bunks, placed side by side. There were a lot of us and very little room. Somehow we had to fit. Four girls, they said, had to sleep on each tier. Four on each narrow shelf? This seemed impossible. But experience had taught us that nothing was impossible in these places. Two SS women guards with whips burst in and started lashing around at random. "Get onto your beds. Quickly now!"

Each of us squatted in one corner of a tier, legs folded underneath. Twelve to a bunk, like monkeys in a cage. This won't do for long, we thought.

But our foursome soon hit on a practical solution.

"Girls, if we're going to get any sleep," I said, "and stretch our legs a bit so that we don't become paralyzed, let's try this idea. Two of us on each tier can stretch out until midnight, while the other two stay doubled up. Then after midnight we'll switch. That way we'll all get some rest. How about it?"

Everyone agreed. We took our places, and the rest of the room, seeing what we had done, did the same.

There was no work here for us to do. It was evidently just a place to stay. Rations consisted once more of a tin of thin soup a day and a piece of bread. Twice a day we had roll call to be counted. For the rest of the time we were locked in our building.

We had been there nearly a week when a rumor spread that we were going to be sent somewhere else yet again. We felt like eternal pilgrims. We were anticipating the next stage in our journey with horror. Judging by the last, we were not likely to survive it. It was still February, and in our pitiful rags we seemed doomed to freeze to death.

Something unexpected happened that night. I had been suddenly awakened by the glare of a searchlight illuminating the parade ground beneath our window.

I crawled down from my bunk and stood beside the window to see what was going on. For a moment there was silence. No one was in sight. Then I saw two prisoners crossing the parade ground diagonally, carrying a wooden stretcher piled high with clothes. They walked quite normally, not at the usual trot. When they were about halfway across an SS man appeared with a revolver in his hand, obviously keeping an eye on them. I went on watching. The operation kept recurring, but I noticed that the SS man didn't turn up every time. Most times he was there, other times he wasn't.

A crazy idea occurred to me. Sometimes, in extreme desperation, we do something so at odds with our normal judgment that it borders on madness.

If we were not to freeze to death on the next stage of our journey, I reasoned, we had to get hold of some more clothes by hook or by crook. And right now I could see clothes in abundance passing just underneath our window. Why not jump out of the window and nab a supply off the stretcher? The prisoners wouldn't harm me. But what about the SS man who followed them?

One time yes, then sometimes no. It would be like Russian roulette. My mind was made up. If my time was up, he would shoot me dead. If it wasn't, we would all be warmly dressed for the journey.

Something clicked in my head. No second thoughts. Do it! I opened the window, jumped out just as the stretcher was passing, and ran after it across the parade ground with the searchlights beaming from all corners. Springing between the two prisoners, I grabbed an armful of clothes and rushed back. They were startled and stopped in their tracks. There was no SS man coming, though I hardly looked to see. Throwing the things up through the window—we were on the second floor—I climbed the wall like a wild cat, shot through the window, and closed it behind me. Under normal circumstances I would never have managed it, but when our lives are in the balance we are capable of many things.

Still catching my breath, I turned around and squinted through the side of the window to see what happened. The next two prisoners were just arriving with their stretcher load of clothes. The SS man was following about ten paces behind them with his revolver at the ready. He twirled it around his forefinger as he walked.

29. ACROSS CZECH TERRITORY

Only two days after my little adventure an SS woman told us we were being dispatched onward, so it was all out on the parade ground to be counted.

We stood as usual in fives. After losing Marta we had drafted Blanka Krausová into our group, the girl who had found the cellar full of potatoes in Kurzbach. We were a good team.

Nana Krásová was in the center position. It was a beautiful, sunny, late-winter day when, in other, long forgotten times, the snow would have squeaked merrily under our feet in warm snow boots and the blue sky would have smiled down upon us on some Austrian mountainside.

Suddenly it happened.

The SS women had just checked our numbers and were leisurely marching back and forth in front of us when, suddenly, without warning, Nana stepped out from between us and walked off slowly in no particular direction, as much as to say, I'm finished with all this. This is not for me anymore. I'm leaving. You have a good time.

We all froze in astonishment. Even the SS women stared in disbelief. They had never seen anything like it. It was just inconceivable to them that anyone would break ranks and step out of line.

As calm as could be, like a sleepwalker, Nana went up to the wire fence separating us from the rest of the camp. As she leaned on the wire with her back, her face to the sun, a smile flitted across her features. Perhaps she was imagining her Hans coming on his white horse to take her "where there was plenty of everything," as she had once described her dream to me in Kurzbach. Then quietly she slipped to the ground and died on the spot, a sheer act of will. The wire was not electrified.

We stood rooted to the ground. The SS women finally sprang into action. They ran to the fence and dragged Nana off the parade ground by her feet.

Shortly afterward we were lined up and told to march downhill from the fortress to the small train station where we had arrived in our much-reduced state just a few days earlier.

There was a train already waiting for us, neither a cattle train nor a coal train but a regular passenger train, with coaches marked FIRST CLASS and SECOND CLASS, with large clean windows that could be opened. Obviously some mistake, we reasoned. "This must be meant for some local bigwigs, camp commanders or whatever. They'd never let us onto a posh train like this. Better be prepared for a long wait until they find the right rolling stock for us."

But we were wrong; it really *was* our train. It was unbelievable. We began to speculate that it was a major mix up that would have some disastrous consequences. But no. It was our train, all right, and we finally got on it. There were plenty of seats for us all, especially now that there were so few of us still alive. Destination unspecified, as usual. As we moved off we really felt that this time things were going to be better. How incorrigible is human optimism!

For a while we continued through some unknown territory, unsure even of our direction. But then we started seeing signs and station names that told us beyond all doubt we were in the German occupied Protectorate of Bohemia-Moravia.

The cry went up, "Girls, we're back home!" and those of us in the coach who were Czech broke into the national anthem *"Kde Domov Muj?"*—Where Is My Home?

The war might end while we're in this train, and then we can go straight home, we thought.

Pulling open the windows, we started shouting to people on the roads and station platforms that we were Czech. But no one answered or waved to us or gave us anything. We must have looked like scarecrows. Goodness knows what they thought of us. But it was nice to be on home ground anyway, and this cheered us. Reading the station names was like following a familiar map. We could tell we were heading northwest.

There was no one in charge of us, no SS guard coming through the coaches, no one to give us orders. We felt very cheerful and started singing Czech folk songs. On and on we went. It was like a school outing on Czech soil. Looking out the window I saw a well-known landscape, the beloved features of my home region. There were my hills, silhouetted on the horizon, my forests. Everything, including the view from the window, suddenly fell into place in the mosaic of this latest illusion. *I am back home! Back in my home town!*

As if in collusion, the train slowed down just short of our station and then halted for a few minutes. Even the station looked exactly the same as when we had left there three years ago. I felt like saying to my sister, "Look, Lída, why don't we simply get out and walk. Cross the track, turn right at the station, and in a few minutes we'd be home. We've each got our own bed there. We'd slip out of these rags, get into a long hot bath, use our own soap, toothpaste, and toothbrushes that we haven't seen for years, and get into fresh warm clothes, stockings, and proper shoes. Then we could wait for the rest of the family to get back. Father and Mother, Jirka, my Arno, and your Petr."

Just for the moment it seemed a simple, sensible possibility.

Indeed, why was I here? What was I doing on this train? It was all so absurd.

But at that point the train jerked and we were again on our way. My dream about walking home evaporated. Soon we pulled into

Plzen station. The train came to rest on a siding behind the Škoda munitions works. Some workers ran up to the wire perimeter. We shouted to them that we were Czech. Did they have any bread?

Someone immediately produced a couple of long loaves and threw them over the fence. The others shouted encouragement. "Make a dash for it! Run away! Don't worry, we'll hide you!"

I couldn't resist. At the sight of the bread they'd thrown to us I jumped out of the train, oblivious to whether a guard would shoot me or not. I grabbed the bread in my arms and rushed back to the train.

It had been so long since we had seen anything like it—lovely fragrant bread freshly baked to a light brown and dusted with flour underneath. We shouted our thanks from the window. They waved to us and wished us a safe journey.

What a feast we had in that compartment! We divided it all equally and took slow bites from it with our eyes shut. Each piece was solemnly swallowed like the holiest of sacraments. We didn't notice that we had crossed the frontier of the Protectorate and were back on German soil.

Again it all looked very grim and uninviting, and our optimism and high spirits began to seep away. To cheer ourselves up we began to tell each other the first thing we would do when we returned home.

Anita's husband, Pavel, was the oboist in the Auschwitz orchestra from whom she had had no word since those days. Her contribution now was: "I shall stay at home until Pavel appears in the doorway, throw myself around his neck—then we'll go off to the pastry shop together and eat everything they've got on the counter."

Blanka Krausová had different ideas. "As soon as I get back to our place in Prague I'll nip across the street to the pork butcher's, buy a whole bag of hot dogs, and bring them home for the family.

We'll gorge ourselves on them, with mustard and salt rolls. Everyone will be allowed to eat as many as he can manage. That'll be a feast and a half!"

Lída was already five months along and couldn't wait for the war to be over. She was as thin as the rest of us, and though her figure was starting to show her condition, her loose clothes disguised it. She and I were still the only ones who knew.

It was the fourth day of our latest journey. The train was moving at a slow pace and making countless stops. We took turns sleeping in the luggage nets, which were easy to get up into. We were now in a region subject to air attacks aimed at Dresden. Incendiary bombs were flying here, whistling through the air with a *wheeeh! boom!* and lighting up the sky more and more frequently.

Sometimes the train would stop for our guards to take shelter until the raid was over, leaving us in the train. We didn't even care if we were hit. Every bomb that went off near us was greeted with a round of applause. But the endless journey, even in a passenger train, began to get the better of us like all the others before.

30. BERGEN-BELSEN

At last, at midday on the fifth day, the train came to a halt for good. The rails went no farther. We all got out. By now we could hardly recognize one another. Unwashed and emaciated, with sunken cheeks and weary eyes, we had the fatalistic look of people who counted on no more miracles to rescue them.

It was a wintry late-February day. The sun shone but gave little warmth. All around us stretched a flat silent plain where only birch trees grew. There was still a layer of powdery snow everywhere, a scene that had always delighted us as children. The birches stood to attention and lent a silent, peaceful air to the landscape. A sign beside the track that read BELSEN, with an arrow pointing left.

I took a deep breath of the clean, cold air and thought: How beautiful it is here. Nothing nasty can happen to us in this lovely quiet countryside. We had yet to learn that Belsen would prove to be the worst concentration camp of all. If the others were the antechambers of hell, Belsen was hell itself.

Finally we entered the camp and saw row after row of low, windowless wooden huts among the trees. At first sight it suggested a quiet holiday camp in a birch glade. They led us on and on, almost to the farthest row, where they drove about 250 of us into one hut. We saw the usual three-tier bunks, each for twelve people. So once more it was four to a wooden plank.

At the time, we discovered, this camp was already crowded with thousands upon thousands of prisoners from all the camps that had been liquidated in the eastern territories. Some had arrived by train; some had been forced to march. Only the toughest had made it.

As soon as we arrived, each of us was faced with a battle for food: thin soup and a tiny ration of bread. It was everyone for himself here. Anyone who expected to find some semblance of order soon learned how useless it was to appeal to reason and patience in Polish, Hungarian, or any other language.

People were scrambling for food like wild animals. Grabbing at mess tins, they took the container with the soup by the handle. In the chaos it overturned and half the soup spilled on the floor. The rest was all gone in a minute. Only those who fought ruthlessly for it got anything. The rest, including those who had tried to keep order, were left hungry. It reached the point where we prayed for German guards to be put in charge, for only they were capable of imposing discipline.

The next day we were shifted to a "labor block." There was no difference: still the same three-tier bunks with twelve huddled together like a human skyscraper. Those on the bottom tier almost at floor level had no room to sit up, those in the middle squashed in between, and those on the top tier touched the ceiling.

Our surviving foursome, my sister Lída, Anita, Blanka, and I, used the same system we had created in Mauthausen. Two of us squeezed back at the end so that the other pair could stretch their legs and get a little sleep up until midnight. Then we changed places so the first two had a chance. But even with the best intentions, we didn't get any rest in these uncomfortable, twisted positions.

The daily routine was the same here as elsewhere. Awake at five, roll call outside in fives for counting, standing and waiting . . . standing and waiting . . . whatever the weather, sick or well.

Then we were marched off for "work," though there was no work to do. The SS women simply led us in formation out into the fields somewhere. There we stood all day until returning to the camp in the evening. For this effort we were supposed to get an extra ration of soup, but didn't. Bread was promised but never came.

We were all starving. I feared for Lída now. How was she going to carry on in this place? Supposing the war didn't end, and she had her child here?

One day in the course of our "work" we came across a barrel full of rubbish and stinking bones, with a little greenish meat and yellow fat still clinging to them. We pulled them out and started gnawing on them like starving animals. No thought of food poisoning occurred to us. It was simply a feast. We swallowed the stuff with relish and left a pile of bones licked clean. When we were moved to another work site after a few days, we cherished fond memories of that barrel of bones.

One day later, on our way back to camp, I spotted something shining in the mud. After picking it up and cleaning it a little I saw that it was a heavy silver dinner knife. The broadest part of the handle was engraved with a swastika. Evidently it had belonged to the SS officers' mess. They ate off silver. *This will come in handy,* I thought, and hid it down my purple-colored sock. It was longer than the green one, which only covered my ankle.

And did it get used! Not just for grubbing roots in the fields or cutting up the odd discarded raw potato; all sorts of things were to be found in the bins outside the SS mess that could be cleaned, sliced, and eaten. I claimed that piece of cutlery for myself and took great care of it. That knife and Arno's tin ring, which hung around my waist and sustained my hopes of reunion, were the two things that kept me going.

One day, however, we had an unscheduled body check as we came back to camp. It was conducted by Irma Graese, the blond commander of the women's section of the camp and the most sadistic of the guards. She immediately found the knife on me, pulled it out of my sock, and started screaming.

"Du jüdisches Dieb! Du Sau! Du elendes Schwein!"—You Jewish thief! You dirty pig! Still carrying on like a madman, she bashed

me with the handle until I thought she would crack my skull. Then she gave me a kick and threw the knife away furiously into the mud. The five following us moved up, but I knew I was not going to leave the knife behind. I must get it back at any price. In the confusion around me I crawled against the stream to get nearer to it. Blanka grabbed me by the arm.

"You're mad," she said. "If Graese catches you with that knife again she'll have you shot on the spot! Let it be, for God's sake. Forget the damn knife! It's not worth it."

She was no doubt right, but I wasn't listening. I edged back through the crush and stretched my arm out into the mud . . . the knife was mine. Graese didn't see me and I had what I wanted. Determination, courage, and good luck. Those are life's essentials.

Time crawled by. It was now March 1945. The snow thawed and turned into sticky yellow mud. Nothing changed from one day to the next, as if no war was in progress. We had our routine, and the outside world disappeared and became irrelevant. We could no longer imagine people elsewhere living differently from ourselves. We were getting weaker. The catastrophic lack of nourishment showed; we declined steadily in strength, weight, and health. Some of us were mere skeletons with skin hanging from our bones.

Worse still, we were all infested with lice. Soap and personal hygiene were non-existent and in our crammed quarters lice were bound to multiply. Our hair had grown back a little, and there they laid their nits like beads on a string. They settled everywhere, in our clothing as well as on our skin, which we scratched raw in a vain attempt to relieve the intolerable itching. Many girls developed weeping sores on their bodies that refused to heal. The sores attracted more lice. We were like a camp full of lepers, wretched creatures whom everyone avoided like mangy dogs. There was no water with which to wash, no soap, no relief. But what was to follow was even worse.

Optimistic rumors started circulating at this point about a collapse of German forces on all fronts. The war was hastening to its end, and liberation would arrive any week, any day, even. We just had to hang on and not succumb to anything: hunger, cold, thirst, malnutrition, lice, fatigue. All had to be kept at bay at any cost by sheer willpower until the end of the war.

But we had miscalculated.

Before any liberators arrived, the whole camp broke out in a typhus epidemic.

It spread with the speed of an Australian bush fire and in no time killed thousands upon thousands. It was a disease against which we had no weapons. In the unequal battle for survival our only weapons were hope and the will to live.

All of us fell ill. Fever scorched our bodies, our heads buzzed, our ears went deaf, we were indescribably thirsty, and, worst of all, crippled with diarrhea.

Yet we still had to go to work. Sickness was not recognized. We deteriorated rapidly. Girls dropped to their knees on the work shifts, fainted on roll call. Continence became impossible. The disease had struck us unaware, insidiously, like a sly assassin putting a dagger to our throats.

Like lightning it spread to the remotest corner of the farthest barracks. There was no escape. Every day the death toll increased. With all communications destroyed, the camp was cut off from any source of supply. Bread, our only food, ceased to arrive. All we had left was water and air. The Germans themselves put the final nail in our coffin and cut off the water. Every tap ran dry. Water meant life. To have typhus and no water equals death.

In our despair we started drinking water from a tub that had been used for dirty underclothing and was unspeakably polluted. However revolting it was, we scrambled for a sip. After a few days even the tub was empty. Many liters of its stinking contents had flowed down our throats and through our guts. Though we all knew the danger, we had freely opted for death over the torture of thirst.

The situation was soon calamitous. Some women were too weak to get up from the bunks and go to the latrines, and their excrement ran down onto those below. There was no one to clean the barracks; the German guards no longer appeared. They had left us to our fate.

We were finally transferred to a building where there was no work duty, the penultimate stage before death. Hardly able to stand, some 300 women were crammed together, one lying over one another on the bare concrete floor. Lída was separated from me and assigned to another building, despite my entreaties to remain together.

The next day I somehow found the energy to go and find her. She was sitting on the floor leaning against the wall next to another young girl with whom she had quickly made friends. She was so changed, I felt I had never seen her before: pale and thin, seven months pregnant, with sunken eyes and parched lips. There was nothing I could do for her, but I promised to come again the next day.

We were strictly forbidden to leave our own barracks, but I could not abandon Lída, and I kept my word. I sneaked back to see her the next day. But the place where she had sat by the wall the day before was empty. Lída wasn't there. Her new friend told me what had happened.

"Lída had to use the bucket during the night and it fell out. She miscarried. She didn't know what it was. It drowned in the muck anyway. They took her off to the sick bay." A stinking hole full of corpses.

I went staggering from place to place to look for her. Finally I traced her. It was already evening. She was lying in a corner on a bare board, nearly dead. When she saw me her eyes lit up faintly with joy and gratitude. It was her last spark of life. She held my hand and would not let go, beseeching me not to leave her there alone. But I had to go back. I came again as early as possible the next day.

Lída was no longer there. The board she had been lying on was empty.

She was only seventeen.

31. CONDEMNED TO DIE

It was April 1945. Conditions grew worse. Hundreds of women were dying each day. Everyone dreamed of some magic rescue, but none came from any quarter. Death was all we had to wait for.

One night Blanka succumbed. She, who seemed the toughest of us all, decided she had no desire to go on. Anyone who gave up the struggle was dead in a few hours. As if on demand, death would come and mercifully end the suffering.

Five days later Anita died. She had not willed it; indeed, she had fought against it. To her last breath she had been buoyed up by the thought of the happy reunion with Pavel when they would go to the pastry shop together. But exhaustion and dehydration overcame her. She fell into a delirium and raved until her lips went blue and she died. The two women on either side of her dragged her by the arms and threw her on the large pile of corpses in front of the hut.

I was the only one of our group left. For the first time it occurred to me that I might die here like the others. I had never conceived of this thought—until now. I was just a mass of bones with the skin hanging in folds like crumpled paper. Eyes and teeth were all that was left of my face. My muscles had disappeared, and because of the diarrhea my intestines bulged out of me like a sick animal. I could no longer stand or walk, but lay impassively on the bare floor amid the dirt and excrement. There were corpses, many already decomposing, in the room among the living. We all looked so similar now it was hard to tell who was dead and who was still breathing. Those who were alive lay with staring eyes, watching and waiting for the Reaper to come around with his scythe.

There was no one to bury the dead. Those few inmates who could still stand would try to drag the corpses out onto piles that rose steadily among the birches—the trees that had so delighted me when we arrived. Mountains of human refuse. There were other bodies lying in the mud wherever death had chanced upon them.

The camp was turning into an open cemetery.

Hopes of survival were fast evaporating. It was clear that the Germans were going to let us die here down to the last prisoner. Death is such a simple matter. Fancy funerals with wreaths, music, and gravestones? No such thing here. A little hole in the ground would suffice, with a handful of soil strewn over the spot where the bones could mingle with the dust of the earth.

Unless help came quickly, it seemed the whole camp would perish. Help from outside. That was the miracle the breathing ones were waiting for. The very last ember of hope still glimmered in our hearts.

32. THE BRITISH

Finally, one morning, April 15, 1945, when I was lying on the ground in my last throes among the dead and the living, I heard a high-pitched cry. "They're here! They're here!"

"Who are?"

"The British, of course!"

"Oh," we answered faintly, no longer with any interest. The moment we had been yearning for throughout the long war years, that shone in the distance for us like a beacon lighting our way, the topic of every conversation, the subject of endless fantasies, the moment not only we but the whole world had waited for, found us as apathetic as if it hardly concerned us. We were beyond noticing the world around us, for all the life left in us. We felt no sadness. We had no tears. No emotion stirred us. Just a final drop of energy kept us breathing, that was all.

The arrival of the British army had no effect on our building, the remotest in the camp. We were all in need of immediate aid and attention. I cannot say what impression Belsen made on outsiders unprepared for what they found there. Presumably they had to first establish priorities—like picking up the corpses that lay around, 20,000 of them. Heavy bulldozers started driving through the camp, pushing the bodies into enormous freshly dug mass graves.

To speed things up, the former German camp guards, now prisoners of the British army, had to load the remaining bodies onto open trucks and take them to the pits. Arms and legs hung over the sides of the trucks. To prevent the corpses from sliding off during the ride, the guards sat on them as one might sit on ears of corn in a cart when bringing home the harvest.

Our liberators had certainly brought food supplies with them, but nothing reached our building at the far end. Perhaps those in charge of other barracks along the line kept everything for themselves. We heard that the sick were being evacuated from the camp to the nearest German military point, Bergen, where some barracks were being used as a hospital. They were doing it systematically, building by building. But we were the farthest away. I began to doubt if they would get to us in time.

Several days had now passed since the British had arrived. But we were not counting in days any more, only in hours. Like the others around me, I lay motionless on the floor in a delirium, mumbling pleas for water, water ...

Hallucinations from a long forgotten way of life appeared before me. My father sending me to the inn for beer ... sitting on the steps and sipping the cold white froth from the mug . . . my mother ordering a glass of red fruit drink with a straw for me in an outdoor restaurant, all cold and bubbly ... visiting some old ruins on a school outing, where a stall sold lemonade and lemon and raspberry soda in glass bottles, with a rubber washer hidden under the stopper ... sitting on the grass beside the path, drinking from the bottle ... doing harvest work, raking the hay ... sitting in the field at noon, the farmer's wife arrives with a great jar of cold sour milk. I hold it in my hands and drink, drink, drink. . . .

I sensed that my end was near. Everyone has his limits. Even the strongest will succumb.

33. ONE LAST JOURNEY

A miraculous thing happened that evening.

In the wall of the building where I lay was a long narrow crack through which a beam of electric light shone from outside. I gazed at it, mesmerized.

Somehow the light turned into a voice that spoke clearly to me. "You can go no further. This is the end for you."

I listened to it, but then, from somewhere inside me, came another voice as if in answer, an eerie voice that might have been the final instruction of my inner survival kit.

"No," it said, "not yet!"

Suddenly I felt a surge of supernatural strength that forced me onto my feet. "Get out! Get away from here! Quick, this is your last chance!"

Where had this burst of strength come from, this superhuman power I never knew existed? How was this mysterious force summoned? Whence did it emanate? Does everyone possess it? Was it the Holy Spirit that religion speaks of? God himself?

I'll never know how, but I pulled myself together, climbed over all the bodies strewn on the floor, alive and dead, and stumbled outside.

Crawling on my knees over the wet yellow clay, I pushed on in no particular direction, away at any price from the barracks where I had stared death in the face.

As I crawled I slurped up water from the puddles like a thirsty dog.

I crept around the corpses scattered on the ground, until suddenly my strength gave out. I gasped for breath as my last thought ran through my head, "This is the end. So I didn't survive, after all." Then I fainted.

Who knows how long I lay there in the mud? After a while I came to.

I felt rather puzzled. That last voice that had come to me from the unknown—had it spoken truly when it said, "Not yet?" I stayed on the ground for a moment. No one noticed me. One more of us or less, who would notice?

It was dark. All I could see was a building in front of me, illuminated. Squinting toward the light I made out that I was lying in front of a Red Cross post with the symbol on the door. I crawled to it.

The right-hand door opened onto a long corridor. I crawled inside.

The left hand door was shut. Behind it three stretchers were arranged along the wall, one on top of the other. I squatted in the corner between the closed part of the door and the stretchers, thinking, What a pity I don't have the strength to climb up onto the top stretcher and lie down on it. Never mind, I am used to lying on the floor. After a while the lights went out and the door was locked, presumably by the last person on duty leaving.

I felt safe. I had given the Grim Reaper the slip, just when he had been standing over me ready to swing his arm. With that I fell asleep. The sound of a key in the lock woke me up. Someone had walked in and switched on the light.

A British officer in his military uniform and beret was standing in front of me. My eyes lit up. Not a German guard with a whip this time but a real Englishman.

My savior, my friend. Or was he? Perhaps I was mistaken.

As soon as he saw me he asked sternly, "What are you doing here?"

I answered him in my best English as if it were my mother tongue. "Nothing. I'm just sitting here." It was true enough.

But he must have had his orders, and he reacted in military style. "You can't stay here. You have to go back to your own block and wait your turn to be evacuated. I must ask you to leave right away. We have a lot to do here."

No doubt he was right. He couldn't have known that my life was hanging on a thread. I didn't have the strength to find my way back. Still standing over me, he repeated his order.

"Please leave."

I have always been obedient and eager not to cause trouble. But something different was at stake this time; my life. I was well aware that going back was a death sentence.

I could not at any cost do what he asked. I looked him straight in the face and spoke to him in a quiet but determined tone.

"I understand what you are saying. You have your orders, and your job is not easy. You have been here a few days and seen what you have seen. The value of human life here is nil. Myself, I just can't take anymore. I know with absolute certainty that if I go back to my block I will be dead by morning. Please let me stay here in this corner. I assure you I will live and you will have saved at least one human being. But if it is against your instructions, I will not stand in your way. I would then ask you to shoot me now."

He stood looking at me and said nothing. Then suddenly his features moved, as if in a film, the military mask dropped, and beneath it showed a human face, full of compassion and understanding.

"Very well then," he said, "you stay here. I shall see that no one touches you. I will come for you in the morning."

"Have you any water, please?" I sighed.

"One moment." He disappeared down the long corridor and brought back a jug of clean drinking water.

"Thank you," I gasped. I took the jug in both hands and emptied it. This was not water out of a filthy tub, or a muddy yellow puddle, but clean, clear water. The water of life.

He left and locked the door behind him.

34. MY LUCKY STAR

It was the following morning. I believed the British officer's promise and waited. The corridor was full of people. No one took any notice of me. Finally, he appeared: my savior, just as he had said. He arrived in a military ambulance that he backed up to the exit and opened the back door. There were four stretchers inside, two on each side on top of two others. But all of them were occupied. Where was he going to put me?

I need not have worried. He brought in a spare stretcher and propped it against the wall. Then, stepping up to me, he ripped off the tattered, lousy, green evening dress I had been given six months before in Auschwitz, threw it into a corner with an extra kick, and wrapped me swiftly in a white sheet. Lifting me like a feather he strapped me onto the spare stretcher and took me to the ambulance. He then fit me in crosswise between the others. No doubt it was against all the rules to have five stretchers in use.

He got behind the wheel and we drove off. There was a wide gap in the door behind me. I turned around a little, and I could see Belsen retreating into the distance, into the past.

I felt a new surge of energy. After Belsen, nothing worse could ever happen to me. I would live.

What had been on my mind that day, five years earlier, when I first heard Fred Astaire singing "You Are My Lucky Star?" Why had I felt such an intense desire to learn English?

Was it Fred Astaire who showed me the way? Certainly, his song had brought me this far. My fate was almost sealed when, in what seemed the final moment of my life, I managed to communicate in English with my British savior. God bless the country that sent him.

When I was on the brink, suddenly this Englishman appeared, stretched out his helping hand over the abyss, and pulled me back into life.

So that was who he was, then: my lucky star.

A British officer whose name I do not even know.

My unknown soldier.

I cannot even thank him.

He would never know how grateful I will always be for his act of humanity. He saved my life.

35. THE WAR ENDS

Shortly afterward, we arrived in Bergen, a garrison town occupied by the British. They took us out on our stretchers, laid us down on long stone tables, and scrubbed us with brushes and carbolic soap to get rid of the lice that were still crawling over us. Finally they dusted us with insecticide and billeted us in groups of four in small rooms strewn with straw. There we lay on the floor, one in each corner.

Although we were safe at last, the typhus continued to work its way remorselessly through our bodies. We were strangers; the woman next to me was a Hungarian, I think, and probably the other two as well. We had no contact; each of us was living in her own world, fighting for her own life. One of them lost the battle and died during the night.

Slowly they began to feed us. The days passed and my consciousness moved as if through a misty landscape. Most of the time we just slept. Then one day word got around that the war had ended. Ended? I couldn't grasp what it meant. It was a day like any other and during the night both of my two remaining roommates died in the straw.

Who, of all my friends, were still alive? There could not be many of them. Nana Krásová, Anita Kohnová, Blanka Krausová, my sister Lída—all had perished. Of the thousand girls who stood in front of the gas chamber in Auschwitz and were sent instead to Kurzbach, who stumbled along the marches and were crushed in the trains, only seventeen survived. I was one of them.

"Zdenka, you will be the only one of us to survive," Nana had prophesied that night in Kurzbach. The fact gives me no joy. What am I doing here, I asked, when all those around me have gone? And all for no reason. What was the point of it all? Whose interests were served? The world goes on, but is it any better than before? Human nature will always be what it is, and the lessons of history will go unlearned.

Now that I alone remained, they moved me to a larger room with a iron bedstead. What a luxury to have a whole bed to myself! But I still couldn't get up. I weighed 35 kilos—seventy-seven pounds. When they made my bed they had to lay me on the floor, as my legs wouldn't support me. It was only then that I became fully aware of my state of health, which I had never thought about when I was struggling to survive. I knew I was in good hands. The British looked after us as best they could. I started preparing mentally for my homecoming.

Who would turn up first? Father? Mother? Jirka? Not Lída. . . . Or would I be the first, perhaps? And then Arno. Where might he be now? What had he gone through and what would he look like? We hadn't seen each other for three years. I felt sure he would come back and everything would be just as we had promised. He would be very pleased that I had kept his ring with me as a lucky charm, and that it had protected me and given me strength along the way.

As I lay on my iron bed, visions passed through my mind of my homecoming and of our reunion, in all its possible variations. Around this time the military authorities at Bergen started to register our details. Each of us was given an identity card with name and number. We even heard they were drawing up lists of people fit enough to be repatriated to their homelands. I could hardly wait for my turn.

Simultaneously, however, another project began, organized by the International Red Cross on the initiative of the Swedish government, to send several thousand seriously ill camp survivors to Sweden for treatment. I had never thought about Sweden. The proposed rescue plan had nothing to do with me. I was sure I would be sent to my own country and could only hope it would happen soon. I started to become impatient. The war was over, we weren't threatened from any direction, Belsen was behind me. Let's go home!

Soon the first groups were indeed leaving Bergen for their home countries. I longed and longed for my turn to come, but fate decided otherwise. A member of the British administration came to tell me my name was on a list of patients bound for Sweden. My disappointment couldn't have been greater. I begged them with tears not to send me there. I wanted to go home, not to Sweden, where I had no connections and didn't know the language. I must return home! Please! But it was no use. They assured me that I would recuperate and regain my health and strength in Sweden and could then return to my own country whenever I liked.

My roommate now was Erna Luxová from Plzen, who had been through Belsen as well. She was not on the Swedish list but would have liked to have been. She sat up on my bed and uttered these memorable words, "Don't be stupid, Zdenka. Go to Sweden, they have real bacon there!"

We were still very hungry. We were being fed only a light diet, very sparingly, on account of our deteriorated physical condition, so the idea of bacon became at that moment quite irresistible. Well, I thought, since I'm on the list anyway, I could go there for a bit, get better quickly, and return home a fit person. The bacon did it. Little did I know it would determine the rest of my life. That yen for bacon was to put me on an entirely new track, a new future, a new world.

36. AFTERMATH

All of us on the Sweden list were soon sent from Bergen to the port of Lübeck, where we were put on a large ship already fitted with hospital beds. On July 1, 1945, we sailed past the island of Kalmar and arrived at the town of Norrköping on the eastern coast. We were taken down the gangway on stretchers. I was so curious to see where I was that I twisted around and fell off onto the ground. Such was my first contact with Swedish soil.

They took us to a large modern hospital where we were accommodated four to a room. Each of us had a bed waiting with clean white linen, a fresh-smelling pillow, and her own soft, warm blanket. It was something we had only dreamed of all those years. We felt we had gone from hell straight to heaven.

We were met by a small reception committee from the emergency service and registered by name and nationality. One of the officials was a Czech woman living in Sweden, Dr. Helena Hájková. She welcomed me like a long-lost relative; we soon became very close, and she later helped me a great deal.

We were given excellent treatment and first class food. For the first time in years I held a cake of scented soap in my hand. In Belsen, after all, we didn't even have water, let alone soap—something to be remembered from a previous life. Now each of us had a toothbrush, toothpaste, and a comb, things we had not set eyes on since leaving Terezín.

Everyone we met was kind and full of compassion, even though they could hardly conceive of what conditions we had come from and what we had endured.

Slowly our physical condition improved and we began to approach normality. We were allowed to walk along the corridors and even take our first tentative steps outside the building in the street. We didn't have to wear the Star of David. No one threatened us with arrest. On the contrary, people smiled at us. Our hair grew in and we could recognize ourselves again. The streets were lively, full of traffic, shops, and activity. It took us a while to get used to moving among normal people who had never been prisoners. Our spirits rose as our health improved and we looked forward to going home.

Then everything changed. Official rosters of concentration camp survivors began to appear. Dr. Hájková had access to them and brought them to show me. I leafed through them feverishly in the hope that the next day, or the day after, I would spot the names of Arno or my family. They never appeared. Not one of their names was among the list of the living. How was I to cope with this sudden moment of truth, for which I was least prepared? How could I accept that every one of those closest to me had perished, would never come back, would never be seen again?

Information and statistics began appearing about the fate of individual transports to the extermination camps. These established beyond doubt that everyone who was sent to the left on arrival at Auschwitz went straight to the gas chambers. That accounted for Mother. Just as my old acquaintance there had informed me, she had gone "up the chimney." And I thought he was mentally deranged.

I also found out that Arno's "penal transport," retribution for the assassination of Reinhard Heydrich, had been sent to Poland in June 1942, where, at a place called Trawniky, everyone was killed on arrival. Arno had had no chance. The tin ring he had slipped onto my finger before he left was all that remained of him.

One day I also learned from a friend of my brother what had become of him. After Jirka's arrival in Auschwitz in the autumn of 1944, he was sent on a transport to Gliwice to build a rocket munitions factory. When the Russian front moved closer in January

1945, he made a bid for freedom but two SS men caught him escaping and shot him.

About my father, I had not yet been able to establish anything.

So no one had survived. No one had returned. Our family had vanished. Even our home, I learned, was already occupied by strangers. It finally dawned on me that I was left completely alone in the world.

Alone in a foreign country, ill, without friends, without any means. All I possessed were Arno's ring and the swastika-engraved knife I had found in the mud at Belsen—my total worldly goods.

I was engulfed by a wave of despair. For four years I had struggled to survive at all cost. I never gave in. Now, safe and free at last, I had no desire to live, nothing and no one to live for. I wished I had stayed in Belsen with the others, Lída, Anita, Blanka.

What was I doing here? Why should I be the only one left? I sank into a deep depression, wondering how I would start a new life from scratch, begin again from nothing, from zero. The only clothes I had were those I was wearing, donated by the hospital. How would I pull myself together? Where would I start?

I found myself a girlfriend, Vera. It's easier to pull as a pair. She had been a dancer in Prague, gone through Belsen, and was now also alone with no idea where to turn. We teamed up and immediately felt better. We decided to stay in Sweden for a while and then decide what to do next. We had nowhere to go back to, and no one was expecting us. Other people were already living in our old homes. Before we could start rebuilding our life brick by brick, we had to face the task of laying a new foundation, inch by inch.

The Swedish government offered to anyone who wanted to stay the right of residence with social benefits. To give us the chance of earning our own living, we were given jobs in a biscuit factory at Kungälv in southern Sweden.

We found room and board with a family named Johanson. They were very kind people and took good care of us. But they lived outside the town, about an hour's walk from the factory. Work started at 7:30 A.M.

We found ourselves on a production line with twenty older, experienced packers. The job seemed simple to us at first. A paper box, marked out, had to be folded in two, nine biscuits put inside undamaged, and the packet passed along the moving belt. The production quota was 140 boxes filled per person per hour. For packers who had spent half a lifetime on the job, it was easy. But we kept breaking biscuits, couldn't fold the paper fast enough, and generally lagged behind. We only managed about 70 boxes per hour, which held up production considerably.

The old hands, who saw us as intruders from the start, spotted this immediately and complained to the foreman. One day he came to tell us we would have to be shifted from the production line to lighter work with lower pay. The job and our whole way of life was hardly ideal and didn't offer any prospects for the future. We felt rather like Chaplin in *Modern Times*. We were determined to achieve the 140 boxes per hour quota. If the others could do it, so could we.

"You know what?" I said to Vera. "You're a trained seamstress and good with your hands, and I've got a pianist's fingers, so let's take a few boxes home with us and see if we can fold them faster. I bet we can do it. Somehow we must manage to stay on the production line."

I talked to the foreman and begged him to let us carry on for one more week. The strategy worked. Instead of going to bed we tried and found a new way to fold the cardboard until we got it. We surprised ourselves at how quickly it went. In exactly a week we were able to turn out not just 140 boxes an hour but 165! No one had ever reached that figure. The old hands, who had felt no particular love for us before, positively hated us now. But the foreman was pleased and let us stay on the job.

It was a drab, unvarying life. On top of the monotonous work and the long walks back and forth to the factory, there was nothing for us when we got home—just fatigue and sleep. We felt time stretching out cheerlessly before us into an empty future, not a spark of hope that anything might change. A deep depression descended upon us at the thought of spending the rest of our lives packing biscuits.

"We'll never get out of here!" I wept on Vera's shoulder. She tried to cheer me up. "Don't worry. You'll see, both of us will end up where we belong." But she couldn't say how.

Then an unexpected thing happened. One day there was a telegram for me from Dr. Hájková. CZECH EMBASSY IN STOCK-HOLM LOOKING FOR CZECH SECRETARY. MEET YOU AT 1615 HRS THURSDAY, STOCKHOLM MAIN STATION.

We hadn't counted on this, a career opportunity falling into my lap. But I felt I had to reject it. "I can't take a job in Stockholm and leave you alone in this ghastly factory! We must stick together. I'll forget the Thursday date. I'm not going!"

"You must be crazy!" Vera told me. "Of course you'll go! Can't you see this is our only chance of escaping from here? You're sure to get the position and move to Stockholm. I'll follow you as soon as I can and we'll be together again."

I had to admit she was right. So I boarded a train for Stockholm, dressed as best as I could. I was scared stiff. Supposing Dr. Hájková wasn't on the platform. Where would I go next, not knowing a soul?

In fact, Dr. Hájková *was* there and greeted me with enthusiasm. We took a taxi straight to the embassy. The new ambassador, Dr.

Eduard Táborsky, former secretary to President Beneš, was await-ing us in his office.

After a short formal introduction he said, "I see you've had a Czech education, and we need a Czech secretary here right away. But do you know enough Swedish to work the switchboard and answer the phone?" I was aware that my future depended on my answer to this question. I also knew that a switchboard was be-yond my technical ability in any language and, worse still, that all I could say in Swedish was yes, no, and *tack så mycket*—thanks. Sheer panic ran through my body. Then the word of advice from my father flashed through my mind. "Never say there's anything you can't do. Remember, if an elephant can learn to walk on bot-tles in a circus, there's nothing *you* can't master."

The ambassador sat waiting for my answer.

I looked him straight in the face and said, "Yes, I do."

"Very well. You can start on Monday."

I returned to Kungälv and gave my notice. To my surprise I was handed a testimonial from the factory as the best biscuit packer they'd ever had. I put my scraps of clothing in my case, bade Vera a temporary farewell, and took the train back to Stockholm. I found a room right away in the Birgerjarlsgatan, only a short walk from the embassy at Nybrokajen 15.

Now my problems really began. My first week on the switch-board was like a nightmare. The language problem made it even worse. I couldn't understand a word of what people were saying on the telephone. I soon learned to repeat their phrases like a par-rot without knowing what I was saying. This was a problem I had to conquer quickly.

I bought a dictionary and piles of newspapers, sat over them night after night and tried to make sense of them. Study, study, listen, listen, talk, talk. Gradually I sensed that I was digging my way out of a dark tunnel into the daylight; I began to understand what people were saying and could even begin to answer in Swedish.

The office work among a small group of Czech women was varied and interesting. We were often invited to take part in official events in honor of prominent people and VIP visitors. Soon there were invitations to good restaurants and new clothes; the world began to open up. The biscuit production line vanished into the past.

Vera soon came to join me and our life started to work out as she had foreseen. She quickly found a job as a seamstress in one of the big department stores. We were starting to enjoy life. We never quite got used to the long dark Nordic winter, though, or the short summer months when long days flowed into the next without any real night in between.

One day I had a surprise letter from someone I had never heard of, a Dr. J. Lederer of Prague. He had found my name on a list of extermination camp survivors and wrote that he had been with my father in Auschwitz for several months. They had left in January 1945 when the camp was wound down, and he had been on a march with my father when he died two weeks later.

Dr. Lederer described how courageous Father had been, encouraging people around him, and said he had often talked about me. It was his dearest wish that I should survive. He was convinced I would. Doctor Lederer invited me to Prague to tell me about my father since they had been together until the end. He said how pleased he would be to meet me.

I knew I should go to Prague to meet Dr. Lederer as soon as possible. Chance played into my hands. One of our embassy staff was driving back to Prague for Christmas and offered me a lift. We drove right through Germany. The German cities had been leveled and, in 1946, were still in ruins. Scorched brick, twisted wire, broken stairways, and piles of rubble were all that remained of people's homes.

Divine justice?

Prague rose before us in all its beauty, pristine, majestic, untouched by the fury of war. First thing the next day I set out to meet this Dr. Lederer face to face. He lived in a large apartment house on Dlouhá Trída in central Prague. The lift was broken. I walked up to the third floor.

There was his front door, in carved brown wood. On the left was a white doorbell with a copper plate above it, DR. J. LEDERER.

My finger was poised. All I had to do was push the bell. Suddenly I decided I didn't want to know anything more about my father. No details about his sufferings, or how or where he had died. I could still see him standing in the doorway, in full command of himself as the Gestapo led him off, raising his hat to us and saying, "Just keep calm. Remember, calmness is strength."

That was how I wanted to remember him.

My hand dropped from the doorbell. I walked downstairs and out onto the street. I never met Dr. Lederer. With this decision I closed the final chapter of our family album and put it deep down into the safe of memory.

Two days later I returned to Sweden. As much as I longed for my native town in Bohemia, I didn't return to my home again until almost fifty years later.

EPILOGUE

The elderly woman who arrived in that small provincial town after a nearly fifty-year absence was still sitting on a pile of planks looking at the house in which she had once lived. Deep within her memory she saw the whole story of her life before her. A huge tidal wave, she felt, had passed through there and swept everything away into a sea of oblivion.

It was time to say goodbye to the past.

She stood and walked a few paces toward the house. Picking up four smooth stones from the ground, she laid them not on a grave, according to the old Jewish custom, but on the doorstep, in memory of the dead: her father, her mother, her brother, and her sister.

It had gotten much colder. She turned away from the house and walked toward the station to catch the train back to Prague.

A man standing on the platform looked up at the cold gray sky and then turned to her and said, "Snow will be coming early this year, I reckon."

A Note on the Type

The text was set in 12 point Minion with a leading of 15 points. A 1990 Adobe Originals typeface, Minion was created by Robert Slimbach, and was inspired by classical, old style typefaces of the late Renaissance—a period of elegant, beautiful, and highly readable type designs. Created primarily for text setting, Minion combines the aesthetic and functional qualities that make text type highly readable with the versatility of digital technology. The uses of this adaptable font range from limited-edition books, to newsletters, to packaging.

≈

The display font is Futura, which was designed by Paul Renner in 1927. Futura is the classic example of a geometric sans serif type. Its original concept was based on the Bauhaus design philosophy that "form follows function." Futura uses basic geometric proportions with no weight stresses, serifs, or frills, with long ascenders and descenders that give it more elegance than most sans serif typefaces. The wide range of weights plus condensed faces provide a variety of ways to set short text blocks and display copy with a strong, no-nonsense appearance.

Composed by Charles B. Hames
New York, New York

Printed and bound by the Maple-Vail Book Manufacturing Group
Binghamton, New York